THE COMPLETE GUIDE TO
natural
dyeing

THE COMPLETE GUIDE TO
natural
dyeing

Techniques and Recipes for Dyeing
Fabrics, Yarns, and Fibers at Home

EVA LAMBERT & TRACY KENDALL

INTERWEAVE.
interweavestore.com

A QUARTO BOOK

Copyright © 2010 Quarto Inc.

Published in North America by

Interweave Press LLC
201 East Fourth Street
Loveland, CO 80537-5655
interweavestore.com
All rights reserved.

Conceived, designed, and produced by
Quarto Publishing plc
The Old Brewery
6 Blundell Street
London
N7 9BH

ISBN: 978-1-59668-181-1

Library of Congress Cataloging-in-Publication
Data:
Lambert, Eva, 1935-
The complete guide to natural dyeing fabric,
yarn, and fiber : techniques and recipes for
dyeing fabrics, yarns, and fibers at home /
Eva Lambert and Tracy Kendall.
p. cm.
Includes bibliographical references and index.
ISBN 978-1-59668-181-1
1. Dyes and dyeing, Domestic. 2. Dye plants.
3. Textile fibers. I. Kendall, Tracy. II. Title.
TT854.3.L35 2010
667'.3--dc22

Project editor: Chloe Todd Fordham
Art editor: Emma Clayton
Designer: Anna Plucinska
Photographers: Simon Pask, Phil Wilkins
Illustrator: Kuo Kang Chen
Picture researcher: Sarah Bell
Design assistant: Saffron Stocker
Art director: Caroline Guest
Creative director: Moira Clinch
Publisher: Paul Carslake

Color separation in Singapore by
PICA Digital Pte Ltd
Printed in Singapore by
Star Standard Industries (PTE) Ltd

10 9 8 7 6 5 4 3 2 1

Contents

FOREWORD 10

ABOUT THIS BOOK 12

NATURAL DYES IN CONTEXT 14

UNDERSTANDING THE BASICS 20
Core Utensils 22
Properties of Protein Fibers 24
Preparing to Dye Fibers 26
Skeining Yarn 28
Choosing Fabrics for Dyeing 30
Fabric Properties 32
Preparing to Dye Fabric 34
All About Color 36
Introducing Pattern 42

COLLECTING YOUR OWN DYESTUFFS 44
Flowers 46
Leaves 48
Barks 50
Roots 52
Berries 53

DYEING TECHNIQUES 54
Mordanting 56
Indigo Vat Dyeing 60
Top Dyeing for Yarn 65
Tie-dyeing Yarn 66
Random Dyeing for Yarn 70
Expanded Dyeing for Yarn 72
Dyeing Fabric: An Introduction 74
Multicolor Dyeing for Textiles 76
Tie-dyeing Textiles 78
Resist Dyeing Fabrics with Indigo 80
Batik Dyeing for Textiles 84

RECIPES 86
For Yarns
Weld 88
Goldenrod 90
Heather 92
Elder 94
Sanders Wood 96
Madder 98
Cochineal 100
Alkanet 102
Logwood 104
For Fabrics
Fustic 106
Weld 108
Henna 110
Heather 111
Cutch 112
Madder 114
Safflower 116
Cochineal 118
Alkanet 120
Logwood 122
Indigo 124
Store Cupboard Supplies 128

MOTIF DIRECTORY 130

RECORDING DATA 134

SAFETY FIRST 136

PLAN YOUR WORK SPACE 137

GLOSSARY 139

RESOURCES 140

INDEX 141

CREDITS 143

Yarns

Page 89

Page 89

Page 89

Page 89

Page 91

Page 91

Page 91

Page 91

Page 92

Page 92

Page 93

Page 93

Page 95

Page 95

Page 95

Page 95

Page 96

Page 96

Page 97

Page 97

Page 98

Page 99

Page 99

Page 99

Page 101

Page 101

Page 101

Page 101

Page 102

Page 102

Page 103

Page 103

Page 105

Page 105

Page 105

Page 105

Fabrics

Page 107   Page 107   Page 107

Page 107   Page 107   Page 107

Page 107   Page 107   Page 108

Page 108   Page 109   Page 109

Page 109   Page 109   Page 109   Page 109   Page 110   Page 110   Page 110

Page 110   Page 111   Page 111   Page 111   Page 111   Page 112   Page 112

Page 113   Page 113   Page 113   Page 113   Page 113   Page 113   Page 115

Page 115   Page 115   Page 115   Page 115   Page 115   Page 115   Page 115

Page 116 Page 116 Page 116 Page 116 Page 117 Page 117 Page 117

Page 117 Page 118 Page 118 Page 119 Page 119 Page 119 Page 119

Page 119 Page 119 Page 120 Page 120 Page 121 Page 121 Page 121

Page 121 Page 121 Page 121 Page 122 Page 122 Page 123 Page 123

Page 123 Page 123 Page 123 Page 123 Page 124 Page 124 Page 125

Page 125 Page 125 Page 125 Page 125 Page 125 Page 126 Page 126

Page 127 Page 127 Page 127 Page 127 Page 127 Page 127 Page 128

Page 128 Page 129 Page 129 Page 129 Page 129 Page 129 Page 129

foreword

Foreword

Eva Lambert (yarn author)

We are surrounded by amazing colors, but it was not until I lived in Turkey that I was inspired to re-create the vibrant natural hues of ancient textiles. When we moved to the Isle of Skye, I set up a dye house in an old steading and SHILASDAIR, the Skye Yarn Company, was born. However, my progress would have been slow, if not halting, had I not had support and generous advice from natural dyer Jenny Dean and chemist Roy Russell. And, not least, the business and technical input of my husband Anthony, now a partner in the business. To them and all the folk who have visited our shop or website and made encouraging comments, I thank and dedicate my contribution to this guide to natural dyeing.

Tracy Kendall (fabric author)

With natural dyes it is always the color that hits me first. No matter how good synthetic dyes are, there is always a gentleness and warmth to fabric that has been dyed with natural dyes.

I enjoy the mixture of simplicity and complexity involved when using plants, whether it is simply boiling turmeric from the local grocery store on the stove or carefully preparing indigo—both able to give such great colors.

Working with Eva has also been a joy; she is such a knowledgeable natural dyer who has traveled the world studying other cultures and their approach to natural dyeing. We are worlds apart: She lives and works on a beautiful remote Scottish island, able to step out of her back door and collect wild heather for free; I live and work in one of the world's busiest cities, London, where I can walk to my local supermarket and rummage at the bottom of the onion box for as many free onionskins as I need. Town and country, but both able to use and explore the qualities and experiences of natural dyes—each in our own way.

Looking at the history of natural dyes and the patterns created when using them, I am always struck by how modern a large number of them still look and how many of the designs and colors have become part of our current design vocabulary. You only have to look at blue jeans—perhaps the greatest natural dye success story ever, anywhere in the world.

When you work with natural dyes, you have to make a connection with the fabric and the color, as each fabric and color requires a slightly different treatment or skill to get the best out of it. And even after years of working with these materials, no two days or two pieces of fabric are quite the same. There are not many jobs around today where you can still be challenged in this way on a daily basis—and look forward to it.

About This Book

This book brings natural dyeing into the home, taking you step by step through all you need to know to get started, from sourcing your dyeing equipment to selecting your fabrics, yarns, and fibers, to picking and collecting your own dyestuffs. The book is organized into four chapters; each chapter is divided into dyeing for yarns and dyeing for fabrics respectively.

Turn to pages 134–137 for important health and safety advice and details on how to plan your work space and record your findings for effective home dyeing.

Chapter One: Understanding the Basics

This chapter includes an extensive list of utensils necessary for measuring, weighing, and home dyeing; instructions on choosing, prepping, and washing your yarn and fabric; and an introduction to color, pattern, and all you need to know to make those essential design decisions.

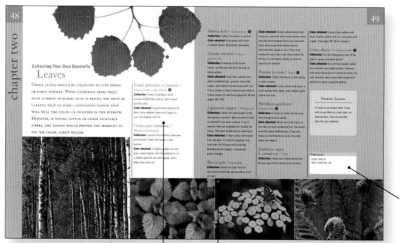

Dyestuffs are arranged alphabetically by Latin name; their common name follows.

This number links each image to its entry in the catalog of plant names.

Chapter Two: Collecting Your Own Dyestuffs

A comprehensive guide to finding, gathering, and storing easy-to-find dyestuffs such as leaves, flowers, bark, berries, and roots. Learn how and when to collect each ingredient and what natural colors can be obtained.

This feature refers you to other articles of interest in the book.

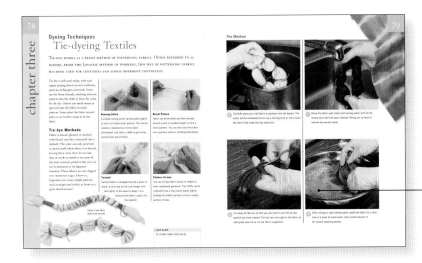

Chapter Three: Dyeing Techniques

Step-by-step photographs illustrate the core natural dye techniques for both yarn and fabric, from pre-mordanting to tie-dyeing, "overdyeing," batik methods, and resist dyeing with indigo.

Clear step-by-step photos take you through the key stages of each dyeing technique.

This fabric swatch illustrates a variation on the core recipe, showing how dyeing time, fabric type, mordant, and amount of dyestuff affects the color obtained.

Chapter Four: Recipes

This chapter covers yarns first and then fabrics and is organized by ingredient or "dyestuff." Match a color from the "Recipe Selector" on pages 7–9, turn to the relevant page, and begin dyeing your yarn or fabric right away.

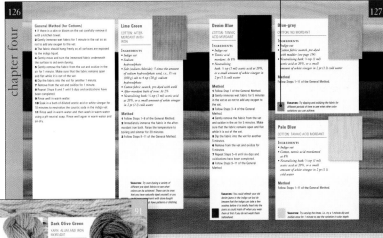

There is a "General Method" given for each dyestuff in the Recipes chapter, followed by variation recipes—if you are looking to dye a particular color.

Each yarn or fabric sample is shown laid out behind the recipe instructions to give you a better idea of the vibrant colors created with natural dyes.

A NOTE ON TERMINOLOGY

Throughout this book, "yarn," "fabric," and "fiber" are used to denote the following:

Yarn
Hand- or comercially spun fibers.

Fabric
A network of fibers, either woven, knotted, crocheted, or knitted together.

Fiber
Unspun fleece (can be carded or uncarded, washed or unwashed).

Natural Dyes in Context

THE EARLIEST RECORDED EVIDENCE OF NATURAL DYEING DATES BACK TO 2600 B.C. EACH COUNTRY OR CONTINENT USED THE RESOURCES THAT GREW NATURALLY OR WERE FARMED OR MINED TO DEVELOP ITS OWN SPECIAL DESIGNS, TECHNIQUES, AND COLOR PALETTES. OFTEN THE USE OF NATURAL DYES WAS WOVEN INTO THE STRUCTURE OF SOCIETY, WITH SOME COLORS OR PATTERNS RESERVED ONLY FOR ROYAL USE; OTHERS WERE FOR PAUPERS.

A Global Art

The Aborigines, originally from Southeast Asia, arrived in Australia 60,000–35,000 years ago. They used soils and ground-up rocks to make browns, reds, oranges, and yellows. In the West African country of Mali, the Bambara people have decorated handspun cotton with intricate designs using mud and leaves for generations; the finished cloth is called *Bokolanfini*. The Picts in the Highlands of Scotland used woad (similar to indigo) to decorate their bodies, which is reputed to have terrified the invading Romans. Native Americans, like many other indigenous peoples, had no distinct word for "art"; whatever they made combined the natural and the spiritual, and the plants they used to color their weaving materials, whether wool or grass, reflected this interplay. Natural dyes were traded as global commodities. Murex shells, used to create purple, were worth more than their weight in gold. Alum mining, centered on Whitby in North Yorkshire, became the first chemical industry in Britain. India, Africa, and Japan became great users and exporters of natural dyes. Today, all these areas only have small farmsteads producing for local artisans and tourists.

Artisan Fabrics

These small producers and artisans continue to use traditional methods of working with natural dyes to keep their heritage alive. They also create new designs and patterns, sometimes mixing old resist patterning techniques with modern synthetic dyes, or using natural dyes to create modern designs and patterns for use on clothing or for interiors.

The skills are taught and handed down by practitioners throughout the world, with modern tools such as the Internet giving a new slant to gaining information. Universities and colleges teach textile students natural dyeing skills alongside skills for using modern digital fabric production equipment.

You can not only buy artisan natural-dyed fabrics to use and admire in your home, but also modern fabrics— sometimes natural sometimes synthetic—with designs made using natural resist-dyeing techniques, but mass-produced for all to have.

Plants for natural dyeing are being reintroduced to gardens for use at home. They are also reappearing on farms around the world as a modern production crop, once again for trading as commodities.

Natural and Chemical Colors

The colors produced from the natural world—whether plant, animal, or insect—seem alive and blend together as in a rainbow, whereas chemically produced colors retain an edge because they are pure. Magnify a natural-dyed cochineal yarn, for example, and you will find not just red, as you would in a chemical red, but also blue and yellow. This is true of any natural-dyed fiber— magnify it and you will see not one color, but a blend of colors.

Couple this blend of color within color with the variables present in natural dyeing and you will appreciate

Yarns

1 Linda Thompson
A design by Linda Thompson in colors of opposite spectrums, which reflect the colors of the Isle of Skye in fall.

2 Eva Lambert
Designed by Eva for those who wish to use their "stash" of yarns in blocks of color, the resulting coat is an original and "one-off."

3 Eva Lambert
Although the pattern is similar to those in Palestinian woven robes, the colors in this knitted garment are more muted than those used in the Middle East.

4 Fiona Moir
This fungi-dyed blanket uses 4-ply Shetland yarns to give a range of pinks, reds, and a yellow-green. It is woven in waffle weave on six shafts.

the expanding spectrum produced by natural dyes. As wine depends on the variety of grape, soil condition, seasonal changes, and purity of water, so natural dyeing depends on when and where a plant was collected, what the season has been like, the water used for dyeing—whether soft or hard, and the degree of softness or hardness—and finally, as with cooking, your mood! It is not an exact science: There is always room to deviate ever so slightly, producing subtle differences. And it is these differences that give a uniqueness to the end product—and that make the dyeing so enjoyable, for there is always the possibility of surprise.

Our appreciation of the differences between natural and chemical dyeing can be compared to music. Western scales are *do, re, mi,* etc.—each note is quite separate—but as world music became popular, Westerners heard music from the East (with its sliding scales) and their musical vocabulary broadened. And so it is with the infinite breadth of color from nature.

natural dyes in context

Fabrics

Isabella Whitworth
This handwoven Indian silk shawl was mordanted in alum and cream of tartar, immersion-dyed in exhaust madder, and partially dyed in strong cochineal.

1 Kimberley Baxter
This piece was made with cotton and silks, compost dyed with leaves and vegetable matter, digital printed, and further marked using Shiva Paintstiks.

2 Isabella Whitworth
This crêpe georgette silk scarf was mordanted in alum and cream of tartar, dyed in a bath of dhak, stretched on a frame, and wax-resisted to create pattern.

3 Isabella Whitworth
This crêpe georgette silk scarf was mordanted in alum and cream of tartar. It was clamped and dyed in logwood; refolded, reclamped, and dyed in indigo.

4 Kimberley Baxter
Compost dyes are Kimberley's trademark: she stains the silk canvas with leaves and vegetable matter, before machine stitching to create a patterned effect.

natural dyes in context

Indigo

Jane Callender
*This design was stitched and bound-resisted
on 100 percent cotton, dyed in iron rust and
indigo, and punctuated with "Ne-maki" and
"Karamatsu" shibori methods.*

1 Isabella Whitworth
This handwoven Indian silk shawl was dyed in indigo—prepared by steeping leaves, adding soda ash to make the solution alkaline, and reducing with sodium dithionite.

2 Fiona Moir
This sweater was dipped and re-dipped in an indigo vat to create a graduated color effect.

3 Fiona Moir
This indigo hanten was tacked together before stitching and wrapping. It was then dipped in an indigo vat about nine times to give a deep blue color.

4 Jane Callender
Dyed with various indigo resist methods such as "Karamatsu shibori," "Ne-maki shibori," and "Maki-age shibori" on 100 percent cotton poplin.

  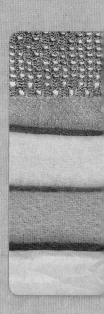

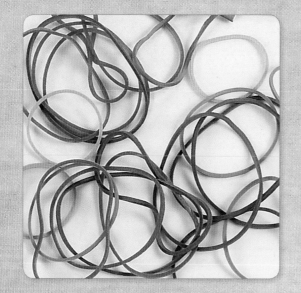

CHAPTER ONE

Understanding the Basics

From building your dyeing equipment list to preparing your fabrics and yarns for dyeing to gathering inspiration for your color and pattern choices, this chapter will teach you everything you need to know to get started right away.

Understanding the Basics
Core Utensils

IF YOU ARE DYEING YARNS OR FABRICS IN YOUR KITCHEN, YOU MUST
BE CAREFUL TO KEEP ANYTHING THAT YOU USE SEPARATE FROM YOUR
COOKING UTENSILS. KEEP YOUR DYESTUFFS AND MORDANTS IN A
SPECIAL CUPBOARD, OR AT LEAST SAFELY STORED IN A CARDBOARD BOX.
DO NOT USE POTS, NO MATTER HOW WELL YOU THINK YOU HAVE
CLEANED THEM, FOR BOTH COOKING AND DYEING. YOU WILL NEED:

Large vessels, either of stainless steel (the best) or
enamel. If using the latter, make sure there are no chips
as the iron underneath the enamel will dull your color.
Brass, copper, or iron vessels will also modify your color,
so avoid them. Aluminum vessels are acceptable as the
alum will not affect your color. The minimum size
should be a 1-gallon (4½-l) container, which will be
enough for 4 oz (110 g) of yarn or fleece. As long as you
can lift them, larger vessels will enable you to dye larger
quantities. If you are dyeing fleece, the larger the vessel
the better, as you will be able to move the fleece around
freely during the dyeing process.

Plastic buckets for storing leftover dyebaths.

Plastic tubs with airtight lids, for storing mordants.

Plastic containers for weighing out dyestuffs or mordants: small, recycled spice containers for weighing out mordants and larger containers for weighing out dyestuffs.

Rods for stirring can be stainless steel or glass, neither of which will absorb color. Wooden dowel rods are also fine. They absorb color, so it is best to have a number of them, one for each basic color.

Scales for weighing dyestuffs and mordants. The best scales are those that will weigh less than an ounce, especially if you are dyeing small quantities of fiber.

Sieve for straining when using a bulky dye material that you do not want to put in your dyebath along with your fiber.

Rubber gloves are absolutely necessary when dyeing with indigo as caustic soda is harmful and will burn your skin. Unless you don't mind stained fingers, it is advisable to wear gloves at all times when dyeing.

Thermometer with waterproof markings or a dairy thermometer is useful for indigo dyeing (see pages 60–64 and 80–83), but not absolutely necessary as you can judge the water temperature with your hand (as long as you wear rubber gloves!). If you buy a thermometer, make sure that it is long enough to reach to the bottom of your dyeing vessel.

Airtight jar 1½–2 pt (¾–1.2 l) size, if you are making a stock solution for indigo.

Plastic apron to protect against spills.

Mask to protect against toxic fumes.

1 Plastic apron
2 Thermometer
3 Electronic scales
4 Plastic bucket
5 Rubber gloves
6 Large stainless steel vessel
7 Airtight containers
8 Sieve
9 Mask

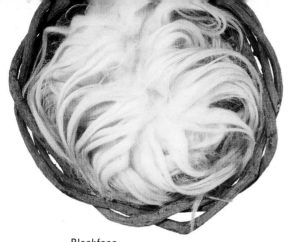

Blackface
These fleeces all have their distinctive features. The Blackface is bred for meat, but in the past some of its fleece was used for carpets.

Cotswold
Cotswold has a fine, long, springy fleece with a soft luster.

Understanding the Basics
Properties of Protein Fibers

THERE ARE OVER 300 DISTINCT BREEDS OF DOMESTIC SHEEP IN THE WORLD. IN THE U.K. ALONE THERE ARE 65 BREEDS. MOST OF THESE SHEEP ARE BRED FOR THEIR MEAT, BUT THOSE BRED FOR THEIR FLEECE ARE CHOSEN FOR THE FINENESS AND THE LUSTER OF THEIR FIBERS.

Sheep

Different breeds of sheep may produce subtle differences in the tonal quality of color when dyed due to the differences in the individual fibers of the fleece. Sheep's fleece is generally made up of three different types of fiber. Kemp is the thickest and has a large hollow central core that makes it resistant to dyeing. Wool fibers are variable, from the finest, as on the Merino, to the very coarse, as on the Scottish Blackface.

For hand- or commercial spinning, the finer the better. The crimp (or springiness) of the fiber is also taken into consideration, such as on the Wensleydale, Cotswold, Shetland, or Merino breeds. Hair, a fiber intermediate between kemp and wool, resists dyeing. When choosing a fleece for handspinning and dyeing, it is important to keep such factors in mind.

Commercially bought yarn is spun from wool only but the wool fibers from different breeds vary in fineness. Pure Merino is the finest and softest, but generally a mixture of breeds has been used in this book—unless otherwise stated.

Alpaca

Alpacas probably originated from the wild vicuña in South America. Its soft fleece comes in 22 colors, making it the most color-diverse domestic fiber-producing animal in the world.

Angora

These rabbits are intensively farmed in cages, often in dim light. Their silky hair is plucked about every three months. It dyes well as the hairs are light and absorb water easily.

Camel

This soft fiber comes from the two-humped camel, which is mostly found in northern China and Mongolia. Baby camel is almost as soft as cashmere. The palest color is a light tan so when dyed colors tend to be fairly muted but beautiful.

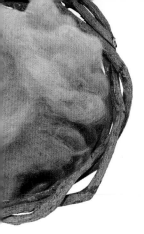

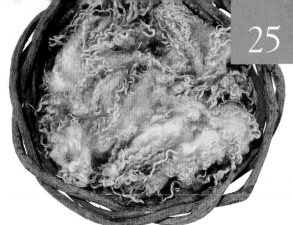

Merino
The Merino has the finest fibers throughout its fleece and is probably the most popular throughout the world for textile crafts.

Shetland
In the U.K., the Shetland has the finest fleece of all U.K. domestic breeds and comes in a range of colors from a pearly gray to an almost black.

Wensleydale
With its long curly fibers and soft luster, the Wensleydale is popular with spinners and weavers and takes dyes well.

Cashmere

This is the undercoat of the Cashmere goat. It is extremely soft, with good insulation properties. Although both wool and cashmere can have the same fiber thinness, cashmere will always feel softer because of the scale structure of the fibers, which is unique to cashmere. Most cashmere comes from northern China or Mongolia.

Llama

From South America, with an alpaca-like fleece, but not as soft.

Mohair

Although from the Angora goat, its name is derived from the Arabic word *mukinayyar*, which means "a goat's hair cloth." The animal most likely originated in Tibet. Central Turkey, near the Angora River, was the center for mohair textile and yarn production, hence the name Angora goat.

Silk

Most silk comes from the Chinese silk moth and has been domesticated for at least 5,000 years. Although silk production started in China, it has spread around the world. China is still the main supplier, followed by India. Called the "Queen of Fibers," silk is soft, strong, and lustrous. When dyeing silk some dyebaths will produce lighter shades than with wool (cochineal and some yellow dyes), others may produce darker shades (logwood, for example). For indigo dyeing, the cooler the vat the better.

Vicuña

The most prized of all South American camelids (which include llamas and alpacas), vicuña has a very dense fleece with an extremely soft handle and lovely luster.

HANDSPUN YARNS

Handspun yarns are more open; the fibers do not lie straight and perpendicular as they do in commercially spun yarn. Also, the variation of thickness or thinness in the spun yarn is not as constant as with commercial yarn. Of course, that is its appeal. But what it means is that the individual fibers are at angles to one another, so when the yarn is dyed, you see the color (remember that color is only reflected light) differently—more intensely, in fact. If you are spinning from fleece that has been commercially carded, called "rovings," the individual fibers will be lying straight, and the resulting yarn will be smoother, although still having the slight variation of thickness. When dyed, the resulting color will be closer to commercially spun yarn than yarn that is spun and handcarded.

Wash your uncarded fleece before dyeing, and it will pick up some wonderful colors in the dyepot. These natural-dyed wools are ready for weaving, spinning, feltmaking, and knitting.

Understanding the Basics
Preparing to Dye Fibers

REGARDLESS OF WHETHER YOU ARE DYEING SLIVERS, ROVINGS, AND TOPS OR COMMERCIALLY SPUN YARN, IT IS IMPERATIVE THAT YOU GIVE IT A GOOD WASH BEFORE YOU BEGIN DYEING.

Preparing Commercially Spun Yarn

Tie your hanks loosely in a figure eight two or three times at equal intervals (see "Preparing Handspun Yarn," opposite) and then wash thoroughly with soap or detergent. Although the yarn has been washed free of oil, it is still best to give it a good wash and rinse.

Preparing Silk

Silk is a very smooth and strong yarn that will take color differently from wool, which is more open and therefore receptive to dyes. Because of this variation, it is best to have your skeins in either 2-oz (50-g) or 1-oz (25-g) hanks. Wash and tie the skeins as shown opposite.

Preparing Fleece

To prepare raw fleece (fleece that has come straight off the sheep) you must cut off all the dirty bits and then wash thoroughly with soap (detergent can also be used).

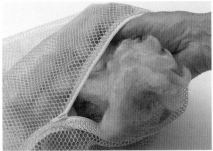

1 If you buy fleece that has been carded and sold as slivers, rovings, or tops, place it in a net bag.

2 Prepare a bath or sink of warm soapy water with everyday detergent. Gently immerse the fleece in warm soapy water and move it around, being careful not to be so rough that it felts. Rinse thoroughly, then carefully squeeze out as much excess water as possible.

Preparing Handspun Yarn

Tie the hanks loosely in a figure eight, wash in soapy water, and then dye following the recipe of your choice (see pages 88–129).

1 Have the yarn in hanks of not more than 4 oz (100 g); 2 oz (50 g) is a better size as it will be easier for the dye to penetrate the fibers. Tie yarn or string in a figure eight around each skein two or three times at equal intervals, making sure that the ties are loose so that, when you come to dye the yarn, there are no white or pale spots where you have tied the skein, and the dye could not penetrate.

2 Wash in soap (or detergent) as for fleece, rinse thoroughly, and gently squeeze out as much excess water as possible.

▶ **SEE ALSO:**
"A NOTE ON WATER," PAGE 35

PLANNING AHEAD

When choosing your fibers, keep in mind the project for which you are going to dye. Of course, you can use only handspun yarns or only commercially spun yarns, but why not mix the two? The effect is one of texture and, if dyeing both in the same dyepot, there will be a slight variation in color tone, which will add an extra dimension. If dyeing only commercially spun yarn, why not add some silk, which will give a variation in the depth of color and texture to your finished project?

If, on the other hand, you have in mind a multicolored project, then you can still mix and match your yarns, but keeping in mind how the colors work together. They can be from either end of the spectrum to give a bold effect or from the same spectrum giving a more subtle effect. The possibilities are endless, and the end result will be unique. The important factor is to think and plan ahead.

Working with natural-dyed and undyed fleece creates fantastic texture and a thick, soft finished article.

chapter one

Understanding the Basics
Skeining Yarn

UNDYED YARN CAN BE PURCHASED IN MANY DIFFERENT FORMS— IN A BALL, IN A CONE, OR AS HANKS. FOR SUCCESSFUL DYEING, THE YARN MUST BE WOUND INTO HANKS. MAKING THE HANKS ABOUT 4 OZ (100 G) IN WEIGHT WILL HELP TO ENSURE EVEN PICK-UP OF THE DYE AND KEEP YOUR HANK TANGLE-FREE. BEFORE DYEING, ALWAYS REMEMBER TO WASH THE YARN FIRST (AS YOU DO WITH FABRIC), TAKING CARE NOT TO TANGLE THE HANKS.

Around a Chair

1 To dye yarn successfully, you will need to hank the yarn. Use the back of a chair to make a hank from a ball or cone of yarn.

2 Wrap the yarn around the chair to form the hank, making each hank about 4 oz (100 g). Tie the ends together when finished.

3 Place additional loose ties throughout the hank and tie the ends together so the hank is held together in three or four places.

NIDDY-NODDY

A niddy-noddy is used for winding yarn into a skein. It consists of a length of wood or metal, with shorter lengths fixed at each end and arranged at right angles to each other. To skein a length of yarn, hold the niddy-noddy and the end of the yarn around the center bar and use the other hand to wind the yarn around the shorter end bars.

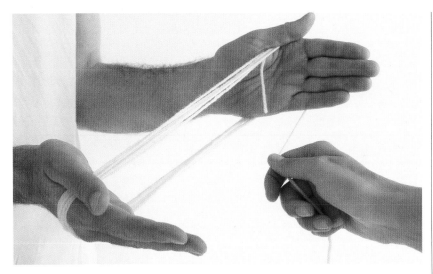

Around a Friend's Hands

Try winding a yarn around a friend's outstretched hands. Tie the loose ends together and then tie the loose ties as shown in Step 3, opposite.

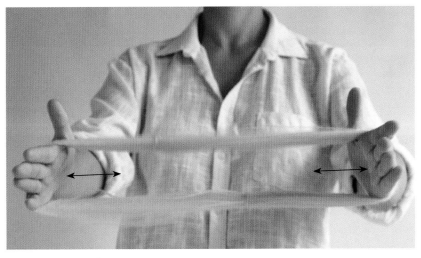

Between Both Hands

Hold the yarn between both hands. Move your hands quickly together and then out again to bang out all the knots and tangles. Gradually a smooth hank of yarn will be formed.

Around Your Hand

For fine or small hanks, wind around your hand. Wind the starting thread around the thumb a few times to hold in place and tie as before.

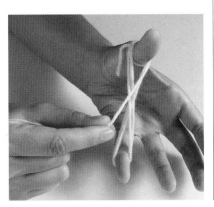

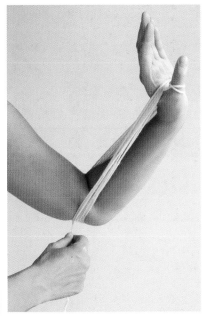

Around Your Arm

First wind the start of the yarn around your thumb a few times to hold it in place. Then wind between your hand and elbow. When finished, remove and add ties as before.

Around a Sponge

Fine yarn can also be wound around a sponge. Add ties to hold the yarn together when dyeing and then remove the sponge when washing the hank.

Understanding the Basics
Choosing Fabrics for Dyeing

THERE ARE SO MANY DIFFERENT FABRIC TYPES AVAILABLE TO THE NATURAL DYER THAT IT CAN BE HARD SOMETIMES TO DECIDE WHICH ONE WILL BE BEST. READ ON TO FIND OUT HOW TO MAKE THOSE IMPORTANT INITIAL DECISIONS.

One of the easiest ways of selecting fabric is to think about how you want to use the fabric after you have dyed it. Will it be for a cushion, a tablecloth, a skirt, or a dress? With this decision made you can think about what type of fabric will be best for your project. A dress can be made from much lighter weights of fabric than a cushion, for example. Some natural dyes work only on certain fabric types and are also better on certain weights and qualities of fabric. Even with fabrics that seem to

be similar in type and quality, the natural dye will often pick up and take better and more evenly on one rather than another.

Fabric Reactions

The exciting part of natural dyeing is discovering the different qualities not only of the dyes themselves but also of the fabrics that you can use with them and how each picks up the dye in a different way. Some dyes are more intense and pick up the color quickly

and deeply, while others—no matter how long you dye for or how much dye you add—will only ever give a pale shade of color. Similarly, while one fabric may pick up lots of natural dyes easily and quickly, there will always be some dyes that it does not. The fabrics below were all placed in the same indigo dye vat for the same amount of time. Note how different the color is in each instance. Every fabric is different, and testing your fabric first will help you to achieve the color you want.

Testing Dyes and Fabrics

You can often do test sections with several different fabric types in the same dyepot to see how they react. All of these tests should be recorded (see page 134). You can then use this record as a reference and the starting point for further dyeing projects.

Alternatively, why not have a "control fabric" for these tests? Dyeing fabric involves many variables—dye type, amount of dye, amount and type of mordant and after-mordant, length of dyeing time—so introducing one constant factor as a stable reference point will enable you to build up a knowledge bank of the dyes and colors and can help you if are trying to match a particular color. While your final project fabric may well be different from the control fabric, it will enable you to make adjustments to the dyeing process.

Vintage cotton edging

Textured basket weave cotton

Fine wool delaine

Heavy blanket wool

Fine silk habutai

Plain medium-weight cotton

Laser-cut linen

Tablecloth linen

Understanding the Basics
Fabric Properties

EVERY TEXTILE IS DIFFERENT: THE TOUCH OF SILK IS USUALLY
SMOOTH AND SOFT; WOOL IS WARM TO THE TOUCH; AND LINEN AND
COTTON ARE COOL AND CRISP. NO DOUBT, THE PROPERTIES OF YOUR
FABRIC WILL INFLUENCE THE FINAL COLOR—THESE TWO PAGES WILL
GIVE YOU A CLUE AS TO HOW.

Wool

Wool is a natural protein fiber obtained almost exclusively
from sheep, with Australia producing 30 percent of the
world's wool requirements. Other animals such as Cashmere
goats are reared for their wool, known as cashmere, but this
is a small selective area of woolen production.

Wool is twisted and spun into a continuous strand from
the short fibers of the sheep. These woolen strands are then
mixed to form smooth or textured, thick or fine yarns for
knitting or weaving into a variety of fabric that is warm,
flexible, and able to absorb water easily for dyeing. However,
wool is sensitive to high-temperature dyeing and decorating.
It can be dyed deep, vibrant shades of colors and is used for a
variety of purposes ranging from strong woolen fabric for
upholstery to fine woolen suiting.

Silk

Silk is a natural protein fabric obtained from the silkworm,
the caterpillar of the moth *Bombyx mori*. Silk is mainly
produced in China and Japan, where it can be patterned with
specialized resist techniques such as shibori. Cultivated
silkworms are fed on a diet of mulberry leaves, but wild
silkworms that produce wild silk, also known as tussah silk
or Shantung silk, feed on oak leaves.

Wild silk is not as smooth and even in appearance as the
cultivated silk, but it has its own qualities, charms, and uses.
When dyed and decorated, silk is able to pick up the most
vibrant and intense colors. It can be decorated easily at home
and can be used in a variety of ways. Whether dyed or
decorated, silk is mostly used for clothing. Silk also possesses
the useful quality of being cool on the skin in summer and
warm in the winter.

Linen

Linen is the oldest known natural cellulose fiber, with examples found at Catal Huyuk in Turkey dating from 6000 B.C. Produced from the flax plant, *Linum usitatissimum*, which gives it its cream color, it is a very durable fiber.

Linen can be woven to provide both cool summer-clothing-weight fabric and hardwearing furnishing fabrics. It does not absorb water as well or as readily as other fabrics, but once fully wet, you can dye and decorate it with the same natural dyes used for cotton fabrics.

Linen is often mixed with other fibers to reduce its tendency to crease. A good source of linen for the craft dyer and decorator is old linen bed sheets, which are luxuriously soft because linen improves with age and washing.

Cotton

Cotton is a natural cellulose fabric obtained from the fibrous substance of the cotton plant, *Gossypium*. It is an extremely versatile fabric that has been woven, dyed, and decorated throughout the world for thousands of years.

There are many different types of cotton, and it is therefore suitable for a wide range of uses. Fine cotton is used for baby clothes and everyday clothing for millions of people, and thick cotton is a useful fabric for chair coverings, curtains, and even camping tents. Able to withstand high temperatures, yet soft and absorbent, cotton is an ideal fabric for natural dyeing.

The range of plain cotton fabrics available for the home dyer or decorator is enormous—try experimenting with fine, thick, coarse, textured, stiff, soft, and even recycled cotton.

Always measure and weigh your fabric before any preparation for dyeing and record these measurements.

Understanding the Basics
Preparing to Dye Fabric

TO GET THE BEST RESULTS FROM DYEING FABRICS, YOU NEED TO PREPARE THEM BEFORE YOU START. IF THE FABRIC IS NOT PROPERLY PREPARED FOR NATURAL DYEING, THE END RESULTS CAN BE UNPREDICTABLE. UNPREPARED FABRIC WILL OFTEN DYE UNEVENLY AND MAY ALSO SHRINK, LEAVING YOU WITH LESS FABRIC TO WORK WITH THAN YOU HAD PLANNED FOR.

Scouring Fabrics

Before you carry out any dyeing processes it is important to scour or wash fabrics to remove any finishes or chemicals used in the manufacturing process. This will leave you with a clean fabric for dyeing. Wool and silk (animal fibers) require a different type of scouring than cotton and linen (vegetable fibers).

While there are some suppliers that sell fabrics ready for dyeing, they are always assumed to be ready for synthetic dyeing and not for natural dyeing, which requires more care in the fabric preparation stage.

Scouring Wool

Wool fabrics often have residues from the oils used while weaving the fabric, and these need to be removed before any mordant or dyes can be applied to the fabric. This helps the dyes to be taken evenly by the fabric rather than in patches or streaks.

1 Make sure the fabric is open and loose and not folded in any way.

2 Immerse totally in a bucket of hand-hot, soapy water. Do not use extremely hot water with wool in case it felts. When hot water is required for dyeing wool, the temperature must be raised slowly so that the wool can adjust to the increase. Make sure that all the fabric is always under the water so that all of it is fully scoured. Use a neutral pH washing powder or liquid. Leave to soak for

10 to 15 minutes. Remove and rinse in hand-hot water. Repeat this process until the rinse water is clear and there is no grease in the soapy water.

3 Leave to dry naturally.

Scouring Silk

Silk fabrics often have a residue of gum from the silkworm or the weaving process. This gum needs to be boil-washed out to enable the mordant and natural dyes to take evenly to the fabric.

1 Make sure the fabric is open and loose and not folded in any way.

2 Immerse totally in a metal bucket of hand-hot soapy water. Make sure that all the fabric is always under the water so that all of it is fully scoured. Use a neutral-pH washing powder or liquid.

3 Bring the water to boil and simmer for 15 to 20 minutes, depending on the quality and thickness of the silk fabric being scoured. White thin silk such as habutai requires less scouring than heavy tussah silk.

4 Remove from the water. Rinse in warm clean water until clear.

5 The water used to degum the silk can be used later for rinsing the fabric after it has been dyed. This gives the silk some of its original shine and luster.

6 Leave to dry naturally.

Scouring Cotton and Linen

Cotton and linen fabrics can have a wax residue that needs to be scoured from the fabric before dyeing. Both fabrics can be boil-washed without any fear of felting.

1 Make sure the fabric is open and loose and not folded in any way.

2 Immerse totally in a metal bucket of hand-hot water. Add 1 tsp (5 g) sodium carbonate per 4 oz (100 g) dry weight of fabric. Make sure that all the fabric is always under the water so that all of it is fully scoured.

3 Bring the water to boil and simmer for 15 to 40 minutes, depending on the quality and thickness of fabric being scoured. Heavy unbleached linen will need 30 to 40 minutes, fine bleached linen will need 15 to 25 minutes, mercerized cotton (depending on its thickness) will need 15 to 25 minutes, and muslin (depending on its thickness) will need 10 to 30 minutes.

4 Remove from the water. Rinse in warm clean water until clear.

5 Leave to dry naturally.

Measuring and Weighing Fabrics

- Measure the fabric and work out how much you will need to complete your project. Allow extra at this stage, as some fabrics will shrink when they are scoured and when they are mordanted. The extra varies depending on the fabric type; some wools and silks can shrink as much as 15 percent if the processes are rushed during scouring and when applying the mordant. Always allow extra in case of mistakes or if you make a beautiful piece and want to continue with a second cushion cover or a matching scarf.
- Weigh the fabric when it is dry. All dyeing is based on "dry weight of goods" or "dry weight of fabric." The quantities of dye, mordants, and after-mordants are all based on the dry-weight-of-goods method.

A Note on Water

Water quality will vary from town to town and from country to country. Natural dyes are often very sensitive to this quality, and you need to know how acid or alkaline your water quality is before doing any natural dyeing. When you know the pH level of your water (see sidebar, right) you will be able to adjust recipes to take it into account.

Old dye works were mainly built near soft water areas, often with natural streams as the water source. This is because most natural dyes take on a "good" color under these water conditions. While it is often assumed that soft water is best for natural dyeing, there are some dyes that respond better to hard water.

Modifying pH levels

No matter what the pH level of the water you are dyeing in is, the natural dyes will still dye the fabrics, but the shade of color may vary from one water type to another. You can dye in a hard water area by modifying the pH value of the water. Some colors perform better in hard water than in soft.

Water is acid, alkaline, or neutral. Neutral is the ideal state for dyeing. Rainwater is likely the most readily available source of neutral water for most natural dyers wherever they live.

You can buy simple pH test strips from any drugstore or natural dye supplier. Neutral is pH 7. Anything above this number is alkaline and anything below it is acid. You can dye without adjusting the pH value of the water if it is one or two above or below pH 7. Any more and your colors may well not perform as you want them to. They will still color your fabric, but it will be a different tone, shade, or depth from the accepted norm for that particular natural dye color.

To adjust acid water to neutral, you need to add a small amount of sodium carbonate to your dyebath water. To adjust alkaline water to neutral, you need to add a small amount of acetic acid or white vinegar to your water.

Strong acids register as red on pH-indicator paper, strong alkalis as blue-purple, and neutrals as green.

Understanding the Basics
All About Color

THE COLORS YOU CHOOSE FOR YOUR FABRICS AND YARNS WILL DEPEND ON WHAT YOU INTEND TO DO WITH THEM. YOU MIGHT SIMPLY PICK A FAVORITE COLOR, BUT IF YOU WANT TO COMBINE SEVERAL COLORS, YOU NEED TO THINK ABOUT HOW THEY WILL GO TOGETHER. THESE SIX PAGES WILL GIVE YOU SOME IDEAS.

What is Color?

There are thousands of descriptive words for color in the English language, but these words can mean different colors, or different shades or tones, to different people. To make the description of color even more difficult, the human brain can distinguish millions of different tones of color, although the retinas in our eyes have only three types of color receptives called cones. These actually detect only three visible colors: red, blue, and green. It is our brain that mixes these three colors to create all the colors we see.

So what exactly is color? According to *The Chambers Dictionary*, color is "a sensation of light induced in the eyes by electromagnetic waves of a certain frequency—the particular color being determined by that frequency." The optimum words here are light and frequency. Within the light that our eyes see—which is called white light—are all the colors of the spectrum. Each color has its own wavelength and frequency, with red having the highest wavelength and the shortest frequency and violet having the lowest wavelength but the highest frequency.

How Colors Make You Feel

How colors make you feel, or how they are used as symbols, is largely a cultural phenomenon. Take white for instance. In the West it is the color of purity, virginity, the color for a wedding dress, but in the East it was, and in some places still is, the color associated with funerals and death. Red, the color of blood, is associated with danger, anger, lust, and, yes, love. When choosing your colors for dyeing, think of how they make you feel and what you wish to communicate.

- VIOLET: the highest color in the visible spectrum is said to have a calming effect, with spiritual associations.
- BLUE: associated with sadness, but in a peaceful, reflective, and calming sense.
- GREEN: in the middle of the spectrum is a balance between the cool colors (violets and blues) and the warm colors (yellow, red, and orange).
- YELLOW: stimulating, inducing happy memories; the color of the sun.
- ORANGE: like yellow, but is more energizing and exciting.
- RED: indicates confidence and makes a definite statement.

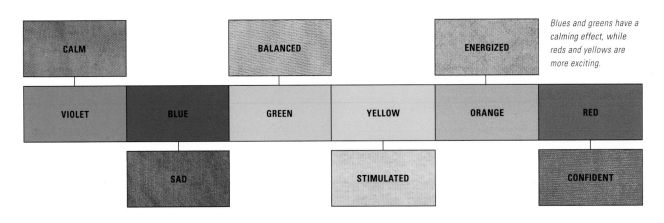

CALM		BALANCED		ENERGIZED	
VIOLET	BLUE	GREEN	YELLOW	ORANGE	RED
	SAD		STIMULATED		CONFIDENT

Blues and greens have a calming effect, while reds and yellows are more exciting.

How We See Color

How we see color depends not just on wavelengths and frequencies, as important as these are, but in the light in which we view color, and how colors are arranged.

The light within which we see colors can make them bright or dull. Hence, a leaf we assume is bright green on a sunny cloudless day, is more muted on a cloudy day, perhaps with a slight blue-ish tinge. After a brief shower that same leaf sparkles and appears more vibrant. By moonlight, the leaf becomes a silvery green and on a moonless night almost black. What is the true color of that leaf? It depends not only on the chlorophyll that we assume colors the leaf, but on when and where and how it was perceived.

However, it is not only the light within which we see colors, but also on how colors are put side by side. Let's say we have dyed a natural dark gray yarn with indigo. The resultant color is a dull black. But, if you put that dyed yarn next to a natural, undyed alpaca, the dyed yarn will appear a dark blue-gray. Or, put a skein of cochineal red aside a skein of undyed white—the red is quite bright. If you take away the white skein and replace it with a bright orange madder-dyed yarn, the red will have lost some of its intensity.

The same experiment can be done with textiles. Take two identically sized cloths—one dyed with indigo and the other with cochineal to give pale pink. Fold the cloths in half, and then in half again. Place the cloths on top of one another, making sure that they are aligned exactly the same, with the four open corners of each cloth on the top left-hand side. Take scissors and cut a rectangle on the bottom right-hand side. Open your cloths and you will have a rectangular hole in the middle of each cloth. Take the indigo rectangle that you cut and place it in the hole of the pink cloth. Take the pink rectangle and place it in the hole of the indigo cloth. You will notice that the small rectangles do not appear to be exactly the same color as the cloth from which they were cut.

Color Inspiration
Look around you, at both the natural and the man-made world, and you will find endless interesting color combinations. Nature is rich in primary hues, while the colors people choose for dwellings express their personalities.

Primary Colors
Bright, full-strength primary colors (red, yellow, and blue) give a happy feel to these beach huts and could be echoed in a dyeing project.

Color and Tone
Here, tones (the lightness or darkness of a color) are varied to create a pattern. Tonal contrast is an important element in planning schemes, so don't avoid dark colors.

Muted Colors
A lot can be learned from what the light does to colors. Here, the slightly overcast sky dulls the hues, but the resulting "colored" grays could be used to advantage, perhaps to offset more vivid hues.

Pastel Shades
Pale colors juxtaposed can look very delicate and effective and are often chosen for both buildings and fabrics. There is a huge range of such colors to choose from.

Variations of One Color
Here, mainly blues have been used, but again with variations in tone. Notice how the dark roofs and white detailing give the blues additional sparkle.

chapter one

The Color Wheel

Color wheels help you to see the relationship between colors, and you can make your own from pieces of dyed fabric, as here. Notice how the so-called "cool" colors are grouped on one side, and the "warm" reds, oranges, and yellows on the other.

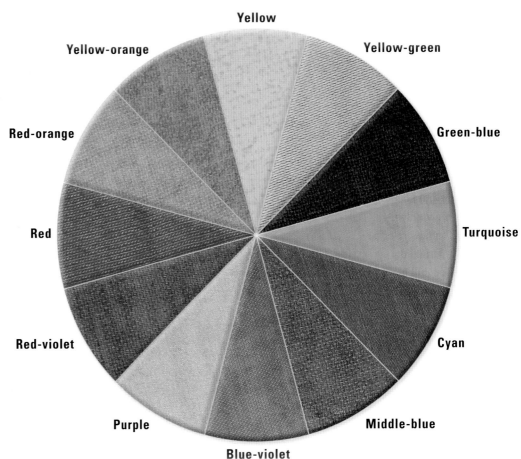

Yellow

Yellow-green

Green-blue

Turquoise

Cyan

Middle-blue

Blue-violet

Purple

Red-violet

Red

Red-orange

Yellow-orange

Color Wheels

Color has been debated since earliest times. The Greeks maintained there were only two vast primary kingdoms: light and dark. Hence, for example, blue was dark with a little light, and red was light and dark in equal measure. All colors were thus described as a blend of light (white) and dark (black).

It was not until the early seventeenth century that the three modern primary colors—red, blue, and yellow—became established. And it wasn't until Newton, in the next century, looped the colors into a wheel, with blue on top going into indigo, then violet, red, orange, yellow, and green, mimicking the proportions in the rainbow, that the color wheel was established. However, these proportions were unequal segments, not taking into consideration the colors we now call primaries (red, yellow, and blue) or secondaries (green by

mixing equal parts of yellow and blue; orange by mixing equal parts of red and yellow; and purple by mixing equal parts of blue and red). It is these six colors that form the most common color wheel today.

Of course, you can keep on mixing and blending indefinitely and get an infinite number of colors. The rainbow, as it merges from one color to the next, is still, as it was for Newton, an inspiration for us all.

Putting Colors Together

Putting colors side by side is on the one hand very personal, but on the other it also depends on our cultural heritage. In the Highlands of Scotland, with its soft light, historically muted tones were combined for tartans. In the Middle East, with its bright sunlight, vibrant reds and oranges dominated. With the advent of global communication and the availability

Complementary Color Palette

These colors are opposite one another on the wheel. There are three pairs: red and green, violet and yellow, and blue and orange. Juxtapose them for exciting contrasts.

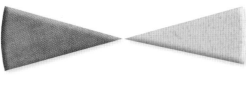

Blue-violet and Yellow
A pale violet works best with yellow, as the latter is always light in tone, and full-strength violet is dark.

Red and Turquoise
These are not true complementaries, but the greenish blue gives a more subtle effect than grass-green with red, which can be overpowering.

Harmonious Color Palette

Colors close to each other on the wheel are sometimes described as belonging to the same "color family," and create gentle, harmonious effects with no jarring contrasts.

The juxtaposition of the three warmest colors is vibrant and exciting, but still harmonious.

Color combinations like this one, neither warm nor truly cool, are often found in nature.

These colors veer toward the cooler end of the spectrum and create a pleasingly gentle effect.

Three blues, ranging from the greenish turquoise to the slightly warmer middle blue, create a tranquil effect.

Harmonious Colors (Warm)

In this arrangement, the warm reds and vibrant pinks at center and left shade into cooler and darker hues on the right, giving both harmony and contrast.

Harmonious Colors (Cool)

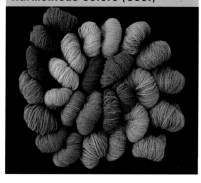

The blues are all obviously cool, but the greens appear by contrast to be much warmer, though would appear cool in relation to red or orange.

of natural dyestuffs from around the world, color combinations can now be dictated also by personal choice and not just by what was locally available.

So what are our choices? They are infinite, but harmony is the important dimension. You can put colors together, basically, in two ways: either by contrast (for example, reds with blues, or colors from opposite ends of the spectrum) or by complement (greens and blues, or colors from the same spectrum). What is important of course is that the colors are pleasing to the eye and that they speak to you on a personal level. Let's say you are going to dye fabric for your living room. If you live in a cold climate, or are planning the project for the winter, then reds and oranges might be the colors you choose.

> *"Color is the touch of the eye, music to the deaf, a word out of darkness."*
> Orhan Pamuk, *My Name is Red*

If, however, you are planning the fabrics for a summer room, then perhaps blues and greens, with just a touch of purple, will dominate. The important factor is that you match what you are planning with where and how you wish your project to integrate with your environment.

For garments that you wish to knit, the choices are much more personal. The colors you choose should be those that make you feel comfortable, and that reflect your personality. Some folk have color charts made for them by professionals, for others the choices might be more haphazard. But the important factor is that the colors you choose, and how you put them together, make you feel good.

chapter one

Keeping a Notebook

What inspires you? Why not keep a notebook with swatches of material that you like or scraps of colored paper that are pleasing to you, postcards you've received, reproductions of paintings, photographs you've taken of the sea whilst on vacation perhaps, or photos of flowers, fall leaves, summer trees, just anything that has moved you.

Perhaps a piece of music you've heard has made you think of certain colors, or a poem you have read—write about whatever has moved you to think of a color. Or, overcome any inhibitions of painting and get out some watercolors and paint the colors or use colored pencils—but it is best to avoid crayons or poster paints as the colors they produce are quite harsh. The important thing is to put whatever has inspired you to think or feel a color into a notebook.

Of course, often it's found objects that move you. Some pebbles from a beach, driftwood in shades of bleached brown, rough dark stones from a forest walk, a squashed rusted tin in shades of muted red, old shell buttons from a discarded faded cardigan, dried moss from a garden wall, pieces of broken pottery, anything that makes you take a second look and think, "Perhaps ..." Put these found objects on a shelf, move them around from time to time to see how they play one against another, and perhaps one day they'll inspire you to dye some fabric or yarn.

> *" Light is the spirituality of color, and color is the corporeality of light. "*
> Al-kirmani

Take a digital camera with you on your search for color inspiration and record your findings in a scrapbook.

Watercolors are the best paints for making notes of your color ideas, and they produce more subtle shades than opaque paints or pastels. They can be bought in tubes or pans as shown here.

Driftwood: try dyeing with alkanet?

Moss covering tree bark: how about goldenrod with copper mordant?

Amazing shades of blue: try indigo vat dyeing.

Forget-me-nots: is this color achievable with indigo?

Beach pebbles: try logwood with alum and iron mordants?

Green-yellow shades: Elder? Goldenrod? What mordants would be best?

Pink tulips: sanders wood?

Vibrant field of wildflowers: try tie-dyeing in madder and cochineal.

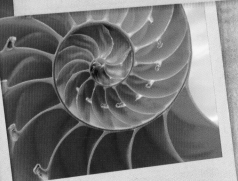

Details of nautilus seashell: try a madder dyebath.

UNITED STATES WASHINGTON 5¢

RESS

William Morris used nature to inspire his designs, often from flowers picked from his own garden. His fabrics were originally printed using natural dyes.

Arabic repeat patterns feature a more abstracted form of design, often using symbols to represent a second meaning to the images such as power, wealth, or passion.

Use patterns from different sources, such as plates or tiles, to inspire your designs.

Understanding the Basics
Introducing Pattern

PATTERN, LIKE COLOR, IS ALL AROUND YOU. SOME OF THE MOST AMAZING PATTERNS ARE FOUND IN NATURE, AND ARTISTS FROM ALL DISCIPLINES AND CULTURES HAVE TURNED TO NATURE AS A RICH SOURCE OF INSPIRATION.

Finding Inspiration

Islamic artists, famed for their use of pattern, have for centuries turned to the natural world and used flowers and animals as inspiration for abstract designs on pots, tiles, and carpets. Renowned British textile designers William Morris and Lucienne Day also drew inspiration from flowers. If you visit any museum, you will find many artifacts with patterns derived from nature. These, in turn, can be used as a source of ideas for decorating fabrics using natural dyes.

Look closely at flowers such as asters, dianthus, and lilies, all of which have the most amazing patterns, either in the markings on their petals or in the shape of the flowers themselves.

Repeat Patterns

One of the most commonly used design elements in decorated fabrics is the repeat; in textile design this refers to the use of a set of motifs that are repeated at regular intervals across the fabric. The practice dates back thousands of years, and today such ancient pattern formations are still used to repeat a pattern or motif on fabric. Even on relatively small pieces of fabric, you can make a pattern with a repeated motif.

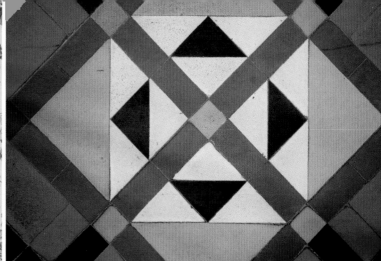

Floral designs are still one of the most common forms of textile pattern, nature producing a never-ending source of inspiration for patterns.

Art deco designs are often repeating units that you can use to inspire and guide the structure of your own design repeat.

There are many repeat patterns, such as the full-drop repeat and the triangle repeat, which you can use to design or structure your image on fabric. You may decide to cover the whole surface or you may decide to use a repeat just to decorate the border. Repeats of lines, circles, crosses, spirals, zigzags, dots, and chevrons were particularly popular in the Roman and Egyptian periods for decorating the edges of clothing. You can also use such bands of repeat pattern as outlines to contain more freestyle forms, rather like the low formal hedges used to contain more informal planting in French parterre gardens. See pages 130–133 for a directory of simple repeat patterns.

Registration Techniques

To achieve a successful repeat pattern you need to mark your fabric with accurate register points. Using a soft pencil, erasable textile pen, or tailor's chalk, you can lightly mark the fabric with a grid or plan of the repeat motif. Masking tape is also useful for guiding you in other registration requirements. Try taping fine threads across the fabric to guide you in your design repeat. Practice will determine which method suits your needs best, and you may find that a mixture of registration techniques gives the best results.

Using Your Fabric

The level of your dyeing skills is another important factor in determining the type of pattern you are going to apply. But your skills need not limit you; how you are going to use your fabric is just as important. Often the simplest spots and stripes, which are fairly easy to achieve with natural dye-resist techniques, can look quite stunning when made into a garment or item for your home— with the added attraction that you have designed and dyed the fabric yourself.

Lilies have amazing patterns both as a flower shape and within the flower petals themselves.

▶ SEE ALSO:

MOTIF DIRECTORY, PAGE 130

Collecting Your Own Dyestuffs

Flowers, leaves, barks, roots, and berries can all be used to dye with, but they can't necessarily be collected in their natural habitats all year-round. The following pages will advise you on the best collecting seasons for your chosen dyestuffs. Remember to collect with care and always in areas of abundance.

chapter two

Collecting Your Own Dyestuffs
Flowers

COLLECT YOUR FLOWERS ON A DRY DAY. GENERALLY, THE WHOLE PLANT CAN BE USED—GATHER AS IF MAKING A BOUQUET SO THAT THE LEAVES AND STEM CAN BE INCLUDED IN THE DYEBATH. FRESHLY PICKED PLANTS GIVE A MORE INTENSE COLOR THAN DRIED— JUST AS FRESH HERBS HAVE A STRONGER TASTE THAN DRIED ONES.

Alcea sp. / Hollyhock
Collection: The different-colored blossoms can be used in one dyebath but should be picked in the summer when in full bloom and used only when fresh.
Color obtained: A reasonable lightfast range of orange-yellows on animal fibers but will dye paler on vegetable fibers.

Anthemis tinctoria /
Yellow Camomile
Collection: Only the flower heads should be collected in the summer and used when fresh.
Color obtained: A pleasing yellow when used with alum, a bright yellow with the addition of tin, a subdued greeny yellow with iron, and a slightly browny yellow with copper.

Cytisus scoparius / Broom ❶
Collection: For fresh use, collect during the summer. Collect flowers only, as the stems contain tannin which will brown your color. For later use, dry whole sprigs, then strip off the flowers and leaves and store in a jar out of strong sunlight.
Color obtained: An excellent bright yellow when used with alum and a lovely green when overdyed with indigo.

Calluna vulgaris / Heather ❷
Collection: For fresh use, collect the flowering tips in late summer or early fall, avoiding too much stem. For later use, cut deeper, making small bundles to hang and dry. Once dried, strip off the flowers and leaves and store in a jar out of strong sunlight.
Color obtained: A good olive yellow when used fresh with alum. More of a mustard yellow when used dried.

Caltha palustris /
Marsh marigold ❸
Collection: Collect as if making a bouquet, including the stems. Can be dried by hanging in bunches outside on a clear windless day or indoors in a warm room.
Color obtained: A bright brassy yellow, which is lightfast on animal fibers. A pale yellow when dyed on linen or cotton. Not suitable for vegetable fibers.

Daucus carota /
Queen Anne's lace, Wild carrot ❹
Collection: Collect in late spring or summer as if for a bouquet, when in bloom. Should only be used fresh.

▶SEE ALSO:
HEATHER, PAGES 92, 111
GOLDENROD, PAGE 90

Color obtained: A range of fast yellows depending on quantity used—the more you use, the brighter the color. On vegetable fibers the shades are lighter.

Filipendula ulmaria /
Meadowsweet, Queen of the meadow

Collection: As for a bouquet in late spring or early summer—before the frothy flowers begin to turn brown. Can be dried for later use but the colors obtained will be paler.

Color obtained: A greenish yellow with alum which, when overdyed with indigo, can give a slightly aqua green.

Galium boreale /
Northern bedstraw

Collection: Collect the whole plant, as if making a bouquet, in the summer. Can be dried but the color is best when used fresh.

Color obtained: With alum-mordanted yarn, a golden yellow; with the addition of a pinch of tin, a bright gold; mordanted with copper, a light olive; and with iron, a medium olive green.

Solidago sp. / Goldenrod

Collection: The whole plant is collected in the summer, as if for a bouquet. Since the plant can grow to 6 ft (2 m) tall, it must be cut into reasonably sized pieces to use fresh. The best dyes are obtained by using only the blossoms and as little of the stem as possible. For later use, dry in bouquet bundles and then separate the blossoms.

Color obtained: A yellow gold with alum but a much brighter gold when tin is added to the dyebath. Greenish shades with copper or iron. Lightfastness is good.

Tanacetum vulgare /
Tansy, Bitter buttons ⑤

Collection: Collect in the late summer before the yellow buttons turn brown. Cut the stems just below the flowering heads but with enough stem so they can be hung to dry for later use if desired.

Color obtained: A bright greeny yellow with alum, but a darker moss green with iron.

Taraxacum officinale,
T. erythrospermum / Dandelion ⑦

Collection: For the best color, only the flower heads should be collected, and collect as late in the season as possible. The whole plant—leaves and blossoms—can be used but the color will be different.

Color obtained: With only the flower heads, a clear yellow; with both leaves and flower heads, a more beige color. Softly spun cotton will take the dye, but other vegetable fibers will not.

Ulex sp. / Gorse ⑥

Collection: This is a very prickly shrub so take care. Collect the flowers only during summer. They can be dried for later use.

Color obtained: A good clear yellow when used with alum.

STORING FLOWERS

If you wish to use your collected plants at a later date, hang them in small bunches to dry in the sun (protected from moisture and high winds) or in a conservatory. Store in jars or boxes, away from direct sunlight.

ESTIMATING AMOUNTS

If you used 100 percent of the dyestuff in your original recipe then once dried, the amount of dyestuff should, as a general rule, be decreased by 50 percent as your fresh plants contain water. The colors may not be as bright as when you use the flowers fresh.

Collecting Your Own Dyestuffs
Leaves

GREEN LEAVES SHOULD BE COLLECTED IN LATE SPRING OR EARLY SUMMER. WHEN GATHERING FROM TREES SUCH AS BIRCH OR BUSHES SUCH AS PRIVET, YOU MUST BE CAREFUL THAT NO BARK—CONTAINING TANNIN THAT WILL DULL THE COLOR—IS INCLUDED IN THE DYEBATH. HOWEVER, IF DYEING COTTON OR OTHER VEGETABLE FIBERS, THE TANNIN WOULD PROVIDE THE MORDANT TO FIX THE COLOR, ALBEIT DULLER.

Betula pubescens or *pendula* /
Downy birch or silver birch ❷

Collection: Collect in spring or early summer without any catkins, which would dull the color.

Color obtained: A good lemon yellow with alum, more subdued tones with copper or iron, and brighter with tin.

Cercocarpus montanus /
Mountain mahogany

Collection: Found in dry foothills, often near pine forests. Collect the leaves in late summer.

Color obtained: A slightly golden tan with alum, made brighter with the addition of tin; a slightly greenish tan with copper; and a khaki color with iron.

Hedera helix / Common ivy ④

Collection: Collect the leaves in summer.

Color obtained: Gray-green with dried crumbled leaves. No mordant necessary.

Genista tinctoria / Dyer's greenweed

Collection: A member of the broom family. Cut the tips only from the bush in early summer.

Color obtained: Good clear yellows with alum-mordanted yarn, greener tones with copper, and slightly browner tones with iron. Colors similar to those achieved with weld so follow recipes for weld (see pages 88–89 and pages 108–109).

Ligustrum vulgare / Wild privet

Collection: Collect the small leaves in the late spring or summer. Take care that no bark is included if you want a yellow. If tan is wanted, then use clippings that include the stems. This plant should only be used fresh.

Color obtained: A clear yellow with leaves only and alum. If using the clippings, then soak them for 24 hours before boiling. Mordanted with copper, a reasonable green emerges.

Myrica gale / Bog myrtle

Collection: Gather the tips from this low shrub in early fall and use either dried or fresh.

Color obtained: Golden yellow when fresh twigs are used with alum; bright yellow when only the dried stripped leaves are used with alum; various greenish yellows can be obtained with copper or iron. If the dried leaves are used, they need to be soaked for 24 hours in cold water, which can then be used for the dyebath.

Populus tremula / Aspen ①

Collection: Collect the leaves in late spring or early summer.

Color obtained: A clear yellow with alum, a green-yellow with copper, and a darker green yellow with iron.

Pteridium aquilinum / Bracken fern ⑤

Collection: It's best to collect the ferns as they emerge in early spring.

Color obtained: When tried with a one-to-one ratio on alum-mordanted yarn, the lovely greenish yellow faded quickly. If you use twice as much bracken as wool, the color fades only slightly.

Sambucus nigra, S. canadensis / Elder

Collection: Collect your leaves before the berries ripen in the summer and use fresh.

Color obtained: A good clear yellow with alum, brighter yellow with tin, and green with copper. (See pages 94–95 for recipes.)

Urtica dioica / Common nettle ③

Collection: Cut the young green tops of the plant in spring, but wear gloves!

Color obtained: As with the bracken, when first tried the color faded quickly. However, with twice the amount of nettles as wool, the color was fast when using alum (a pale buff yellow) or copper (a grayish yellow).

STORING LEAVES

It's best to use leaves fresh. If you wish to use them at a later date, try freezing them. This will possibly alter the color obtained.

▶ **SEE ALSO:**

ELDER, PAGE 94
WELD, PAGES 88, 108

Collecting Your Own Dyestuffs
Barks

As a general rule, barks should be collected in late winter or spring when the sap has risen, as the color substance in the bark should be at its best then. When collecting bark, do not strip it off in a circle around the trunk as this will kill the tree. It's best to collect here and there so the tree can heal its wounds. Because the barks are rich in tannin, they are suitable for dyeing vegetable fibers. But even with animal fibers, mordanting is unnecessary, although the colors obtained will generally be in the tan to brown range. The use of mordants will, in most cases, widen your range of colors.

Alnus glutinosa / Alder

Collection: Collect the bark during the summer but use twice as much bark as the fiber to be dyed.

Color obtained: Without a mordant, a golden tan. A combination of copper and iron added toward the end of the dyeing will produce a greenish black. The addition of tin will produce a bright gold.

Betula sp. / Birch ❷

Collection: The bark should be peeled off in strips lengthwise. Take care not to strip off in a circle. The inner bark produces better colors. Collect in summer.

Color obtained: A fairly neutral tan when used at a two-to-one ratio.

Cercocarpus montanus / Mountain mahogany

Collection: Strip bark in small sections during late summer.

Color obtained: Used at a ratio of two to one, a tan results without mordant; more golden or khaki tones when used with mordants.

Fraxinus excelsior / Ash ③

Collection: Collect during summer.

Color obtained: Without a mordant, a tan; but with alum a more yellowish tan.

Maclura pomifera / Osage orange

Collection: Collect in late spring or summer months.

Color obtained: Without a mordant, a drab tan results; with copper, a tan green; with alum, a khaki color—used during World War I for dyeing uniforms.

Pyrus malus / Apple

Collection: Collect in late spring or summer.

Color obtained: Without a mordant, a pale yellow-brown; with alum-mordanted yarn, a more golden brown develops.

Querqus sp. / Oak ④

Collection: Gather bark, acorns, and galls during late summer. The galls are especially rich in tannin and can be used on their own as a mordant, but they will brown colors.

Color obtained: Without a mordant and with a ratio of two to one, a good tan; with alum, a more yellowish tan; with copper, a greenish brown; and with iron, a dark gray.

Salix sp. / Willow ⑤

Collection: Rather than the bark, which is difficult to peel, cut twigs (leaves can be attached) in late spring or early summer.

Color obtained: Without a mordant, a pale yellow; with alum, the yellow is brighter; and with the addition of a pinch of tin, even brighter. Both copper and iron will green the yellow.

STORING BARK

If you want to save the bark, break into small pieces or pulverize and place it in your oven at the lowest temperature— about 200°F (100°C). Check every half hour. When the bark crumbles easily, cool and store in jars out of bright light.

chapter two

Collecting Your Own Dyestuffs

Roots

GENERALLY, ROOTS MUST BE DUG UP IN LATE FALL WHEN THE PLANT IS DYING BACK. IF YOU DON'T WANT TO KILL OFF THE PLANT, YOU WILL HAVE TO DIG VERY CAREFULLY, TRYING NOT TO DISTURB THE CENTRAL MAIN ROOT AND JUST CHOPPING OFF SOME OF THE ANCILLARY ONES. THE COLORS FROM THE LATTER WON'T BE AS INTENSE AS THOSE TAKEN FROM THE THICKER AND MAIN ROOTS.

Galium verum, G. boreale /
Lady's bedstraw, northern bedstraw ①

Collection: A member of the madder family Rubiaceae, *Galium verum* is found on the west coast of Scotland, while *Galium boreale* likes moist places in mountainous areas in the United States and Canada. Dig up in late summer or early fall. The roots must be washed in warm or hot water and, for best results, the bark, or outer layer, removed from the roots as the red coloring agent is only in the bark.

Color obtained: It's rather a long process but the final result when using equal amounts of root bark and alum-mordanted fiber is a pinkish red.

Iris pseudacorus / Yellow iris
Collection: Found in damp places, the roots should be dug up once the flowers have turned brown during the summer.
Color obtained: Once washed, chopped, and boiled, alum-mordanted yarn will produce steel blue or gray. If copper is introduced before the wool is entered into the dyebath and simmered for two or three hours, a good black should result.

Filipendula ulmaria /
Meadowsweet
Collection: Collect the roots in spring, before the flowers open.
Color obtained: A reasonable black if equal amounts of roots and wool are used. No mordant is necessary but, according to one nineteenth-century recipe from the Outer Hebrides, the addition of stale urine at the end of the dyeing will produce a better black. Try a solution of one part ammonia to two parts of water instead!

STORING ROOTS

Roots can be dried in strong sunlight or placed in a low oven at 200°F (100°C) and checked after an hour. If they break easily then they are done. If not, dry in the oven a further half hour. Store in jars or paper bags away from strong light.

Collecting Your Own Dyestuffs

Berries

BERRIES, LIKE GRASS OR BEETROOT, WILL STAIN YOUR HANDS AND YOUR CLOTHES. BUT ONCE THEY ARE BOILED, THE COLOR CHANGES. GENERALLY, THE RESULTANT BLUE OR PURPLE IS QUITE FUGITIVE—LOVELY AND BRIGHT INITIALLY, BUT FADING QUICKLY TO A PUCE COLOR. HOWEVER, THIS MAY BE BECAUSE MY LOCAL WATER IS VERY SOFT. SO EXPERIMENT! IN YOUR AREA IT MIGHT BE DIFFERENT. THE BERRY-BEARING PLANTS BELOW HAVE GIVEN COLORS THAT WERE REASONABLY FAST.

STORING BERRIES

Best used fresh and crushed before soaking or boiling. For future use, berries can be dried in bright sunlight or in a very low oven at 200°F (100°C) for half an hour. If they crumble easily then they can be stored. If not, return to the oven and check every 15 minutes or so. Store in jars out of bright light. They can also be frozen whole. In fact, if you have berries in your freezer that have gone past their sell-by date, try them for dyeing.

Hedera helix / Ivy ❶

Collection: Not all ivies berry freely; rummage in the leaves to find the clusters. Pick in late winter or early spring when they are at their blackest.

Color obtained: You will need twice as many berries (in weight) as the fiber you wish to dye. Soak the berries overnight then boil for two hours. No mordant is necessary for a yellow-green; for black, add iron.

Sambucus nigra / Elder ❷

Collection: Collect the berries in late summer or early fall when they are a dark purple.

Color obtained : You will need twice as many berries (in weight) as the fiber you wish to dye. The colors are not very lightfast. When using fresh berries, the colors are in the light purple range; if using dried berries, the colors tend to be in the beige range.

Vaccinium sp. / Blueberry, bilberry, blaeberry ❸

Collection: Collect the berries in late summer. Try to refrain from eating them as you need a one-to-one ratio!

Color obtained: Deep purple.

CHAPTER THREE

Dyeing Techniques

There are numerous different dyeing techniques that can be used for dyeing fabrics and yarns. Some countries or regions have their own specialized techniques that take into account the local cultural and traditional heritage of that area. You can mix techniques together to add different patterns or colors to a dyeing project giving a new and exciting twist to your fabric or yarn.

Dyeing Techniques
Mordanting

THE WORD "MORDANT" COMES FROM THE FRENCH *mordre*, MEANING TO BITE OR BITE INTO. AND THAT IS WHAT THE MORDANT DOES—IT HELPS THE DYESTUFF BITE INTO (OR BIND THE COLOR TO) YOUR YARN OR FABRIC. IN ORDER TO MAKE YOUR COLORS LIGHT- AND WASH-FAST, IT IS ESSENTIAL THAT YOU USE A MORDANT, WHICH TENDS TO BE METAL SALTS, TO PREPARE YOUR YARN AND FABRIC FOR DYEING. THE EXCEPTIONS ARE SUBSTANTIVE DYES WHICH ARE GENERALLY FROM LICHENS, RECIPES FOR WHICH ARE NOT INCLUDED IN THIS BOOK AS MANY TYPES ARE PROTECTED.

Types of Mordant

Chrome (potassium dichromate) is given as a mordant in many books. However, it is not only a poison (and if poured down the sink contaminates the environment) but also an irritant. The use of formic acid with chrome can almost eliminate these adverse effects, but even so, there seems to be little advantage to using it as generally the colors obtained are similar to those when copper is used. There are no recipes using chrome in this book. The main mordants used are alum, copper, iron, and tin, which are introduced opposite and over the page. The quantities of the mordants are given as percentages, as are the dyestuffs. The conversion chart (see page 135) will enable you to calculate the amounts you will need.

Exhaust Baths

It is possible to mordant and dye in the same dyebath. If, for instance, you dye with cochineal and, when you have taken out your yarn, the dyebath still has a lot of color left in it, this is called the exhaust bath. It can, if other dyestuffs are added, be used again to give another variant of the original red from cochineal (see page 72). However, if you have mordanted with copper in your first dyebath, this will affect your resulting color. More importantly, the mordanting process, if done separately, is more effective. When you mordant, it is essential that you rinse your fiber well so that when you come to dyeing the color is absorbed evenly.

ANCIENT MORDANTS

Before mordants became available in powdered form, people used whatever was at hand to fix their colors—local clays, certain plants, wood ash (which is still used in parts of South America and Africa), and urine. Urine was used to fix the colors for Harris tweed until the late eighteenth century, and possibly later. In the Outer Hebrides some of the houses had a tub outside for the men to use— for their urine was considered stronger than female urine. A few years ago, to recreate original recipes, a local bar decided to collect urine from their male customers, but when it was tried in the recipes, the urine was too adulterated with beer to be effective! Ammonia is a better and more stable option.

Alum *(potassium aluminum sulphate)*

Alum is the most commonly used mordant and does not affect the color tone. It is generally used in conjunction with cream of tartar, as this aids in permanently fixing the alum to the fiber; it also brightens some colors.

After you have mordanted the yarn or fabric, it is essential to rinse it well in water to remove all the loosely attached mordant. If you do not, then some of the dye will not get absorbed by the fiber which could result in uneven dyeing.

The technique is demonstrated below with yarn. Alum-mordanted yarn is used in the madder recipes (see pages 98–99) as this will give a better color. When you have mordanted the fiber, rinse it well, squeeze out some of the excess water, and place the wet fiber in a plastic bag for three days. When you are ready to dye, make sure the fiber is still damp. Alum-mordanted fiber, if left to dry, is very difficult to wet evenly, so make sure that you do not let it dry out. If you are not going to dye with it immediately, it is best to leave it in a plastic bag until you are ready.

Ingredients
- *8% alum*
- *6% cream of tartar*

The Method

1 Dissolve the alum and cream of tartar in warm water in the mordanting vessel.

2 Add cold water, then add the fiber, making sure it can move freely in the vessel to ensure even uptake of the mordant.

3 Slowly bring to the boil over a period of no less than one hour. Simmer for 30 to 45 minutes. Let the bath cool. Remove the fiber and either dye immediately or store in a plastic bag.

▶ SEE ALSO:
"MORDANTING FABRICS," PAGE 59

chapter three

Copper *(copper sulphate)*

Copper is mildly poisonous so it must be stored and handled carefully (wear rubber gloves if you are a beginner). However, with the addition of vinegar, smaller quantities of copper can be used, which eliminates almost all the copper residue in the exhaust bath. Copper is especially useful for greening most yellows—although it can also brown others (50% onionskins with copper gives a lovely rich tan).

INGREDIENTS
- *2% copper sulphate*
- *4% vinegar*

The Method

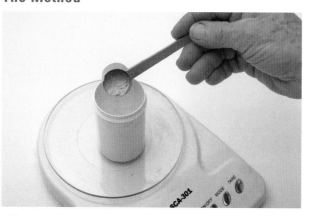

1

Carefully weigh out your copper and mix with warm water in a small container until the copper has dissolved. Add it to your dyepot that has been filled with enough water to cover the yarn to be mordanted. Add vinegar and stir thoroughly.

2

Place yarn to be mordanted in a separate pot of warm water and thoroughly wet it out, then squeeze dry.

3

Place yarn in dyepot and slowly bring to a simmer over half an hour, then let simmer for a further half hour.

4

Let your dyepot cool and then carefully lift out your yarn, squeeze out the excess moisture, and use immediately in your dye recipe.

Iron *(ferrous sulphate)*

Iron has been used as a mordant for centuries. Rusty nails were put into the dyepot or sometimes a solution called iron buff was made by soaking rusty metal in vinegar or soured beer to dull colors. However, iron can affect fibers adversely by making them coarse and can "bronze" certain darker colors. The recipes included only call for it to be used as an additive in "saddening," or darkening, colors; no pre-mordanting with iron is necessary.

INGREDIENTS
- *5% iron or, if dyeing only a small amount of yarn, a pinch*

The Method
Follow the directions given in the individual recipes (pages 88–129).

Tin *(stannous chloride)*

Tin is mildy poisonous so should be stored and used safely. It can make the wool brittle so must be used sparingly, which is why it is only used as an additive in the recipe section—to brighten colors, not as a mordant.

INGREDIENTS
- *3% tin or, if dyeing a small amount of yarn, a pinch*

The Method
Follow the directions given in the individual recipes (pages 88–129).

MORDANTING FABRICS

The chemicals and amounts used to mordant yarns are the same as for fabrics. The main differences can be in the timing and the handling, especially for lengths of fabric as opposed to yarns.

Nearly all fabric will have started its life as a yarn. This means that some of the finishes associated with yarns and yarn dyeing are not found in fabrics. Many silk fabrics, for example, no longer have any gum on them from the silkworms and many cottons and linens do not have any wax from the spinning process. Manufacturers treat fabrics to give them a certain luster, "finish," or "handle," as it is commonly known. These finishes must all be removed before you use a mordant.

Mordant problems
- *If the fabric has a tight knit or weave structure, it can be difficult to mordant it properly because the mordant does not fully penetrate all the way through the fabric. Leaving the fabric in the water for an extra 5 to 10 minutes solves this.*
- *Fabrics in water are much more inclined to trap air in some areas. Pockets of fabric then rise above the surface, which means they do not have close contact with the mordant dissolved in the water. Fabrics can also be inclined to fold and bunch up underwater, making it harder to mordant them fully and evenly. Stir the fabrics frequently when they are being treated with a mordant to solve both of these problems.*
- *If the fabric has been scoured well, it will "wet out" enough to sink to the bottom of the pot and not rise in sections above the waterline.*
- *If the fabric is "wetted out" (washed and scoured) well, it will be less inclined to tangle or bunch up at the bottom of the pot.*
- *Always be prepared to spend time watching and stirring your fabrics when dyeing them. Evenly treating fabrics with a mordant bath will help make sure that they dye. It can seem like watching paint dry, but it does pay dividends later.*

Dyeing Techniques
Indigo Vat Dyeing

INDIGO DYEING HAS A COLORFUL AND ANCIENT HISTORY, DATING BACK TO AT LEAST 2500 B.C., WHICH IS REMARKABLE CONSIDERING THE COMPLICATED AND LENGTHY PROCESS INVOLVED.

There are at least 40 different varieties of indigo plants in the pea family that contain the chemical indican, which is what colors the fibers. Woad, although of the cabbage family, has indican—but the resulting blues are not as intense as those from indigo.

There are two methods of dyeing with indigo. If you are dyeing small quantities, make a stock solution which can be saved if covered carefully. If you are dyeing larger quantities, a single vat can be prepared and, if not exhausted, saved for days and reheated—or topped up with water and the addition of indigo, caustic soda, and hydros in proportion to the amount of water.

Preparing to Dye with Indigo

Indigo leaves are fermented then dried and ground into a powder, which is its most common form. However, the indigo powder will not dissolve in water unless the water is alkaline, thus caustic soda must be added. This dissolved indigo blue will not stick to your fibers unless the indigo solution is reduced—i.e., all oxygen removed. This is done by the addition of hydros (sodium dithionite or sodium hydrosulphate), which changes the indigo blue to what is called indigo white but is actually a clear yellow. Once the wetted and squeezed fiber has been introduced into the yellow vat (which may form a blue skin at the top where it comes in contact with oxygen from the air) and then carefully taken out, the oxygen in the air turns the emerging fiber from yellow to green to turquoise to blue—in seconds. Pure magic.

Things to Note

- The recipes in this book all use natural indigo. If you are using synthetic indigo, which is much stronger than natural indigo, only half the amount of indigo powder should be used.
- The indigo dye vat is prepared in the same way regardless of whether you are dyeing yarn or fabric.
- Always add caustic soda and hydros to water, never the other way around as they generate heat and could explode.
- Animal fibers do not like caustic soda so use sparingly.
- Vegetable fibers do not generally like hydros (which gives most animal fibers a softer feel).
- It is best to have a separate dye vessel for indigo use only.
- All liquid measures are given in U.S. gallons and pints with metric measurements in parentheses. (Note that 1.7 British pints = 1 liter and 1 British gallon = 4.54 liters).

POPULAR MYTHS AND LEGENDS

There are many folk tales about the origin of indigo dyeing, especially in Africa where it is so popular. A Liberian tale tells of people breaking off pieces of the sky to eat—as food for the heart. In one digested version, a young woman went to a sacred spot by a river with her baby to cook some rice. She placed her baby on a white cloth to sleep underneath some indigo leaves, lit a fire, placed a pot over it, and sat looking at the sky waiting for the water to boil. The blue of the sky was so intense that she wished for the blue to come to her, so she broke off a piece of the sky and ate it. She felt the blue inside her but it was paler than the sky's blue. Jealous of the sky, she broke off another, larger piece and ate that until she too fell asleep. When the woman awoke, her rice had burned and her baby had rolled off the cotton cloth and was lying face down on the earth, dead. On the cloth where the baby had lain, there was a blue stain. A spirit came to her and cautioned that now the blue of the sky had come to earth in the form of indigo, the sky would lift high beyond anyone's reach.

The Stock Solution Method

A stock solution is ideal for dyeing small quantities and is quicker—the whole process can be done in one day from making the stock solution to dyeing the fiber.

Ingredients
- *2 oz (60 g) natural indigo powder*
- *2 oz (60 g) hydros*
- *3 oz (90 g) caustic soda*

Preparing the Stock Solution

1

Put 2 pt (1 l) warm water—no hotter than 120°F (49°C)—into a glass jar. Slowly add the caustic soda, stirring constantly to make sure it is totally dissolved.

2

Wear rubber gloves for the rest of the steps in this method. Now add the indigo, again stirring constantly. The indigo may take two or three minutes to dissolve.

3

Add the hydros and gently stir. The mixture should quickly develop a coppery tone, indicating that reduction has begun.

4

Cover the jar (a screw-top lid is best), wrap it in some cloth, and place it in a pot of warm water for half an hour or more. You can add warm water to the pot if the water cools.

5

Check your solution after 30 minutes or so by dipping in a glass rod, which should come out dripping a clear yellow. If there are solid blue specks on the rod, reduction has not been completed. Cover the jar and keep warm for a further 30 minutes or so, then test again. The stock solution can be kept for several weeks. If it becomes blue or green, heat gently and add more hydros, stirring carefully.

▶ **SEE ALSO:**
RESIST DYEING FABRICS WITH INDIGO, PAGES 80–83

Preparing the Vat

1

Place the vat on newspapers and fill it with 2 gal (8 l) of warm water—no hotter than 140°F (60°C). Add 2 oz (60 g) ordinary table salt and stir thoroughly.

2

Now add 1 tbsp caustic soda and a squirt of detergent (this helps the indigo to take evenly).

3

Gently stir, add 2 tbsp hydros, and gently stir again. Cover the vat and wrap an old towel around it to keep it warm. Leave for 15–30 minutes.

4

Check your temperature to make sure the vat never goes above 140°F (60°C) or below 95°F (40°C).

5

Add half of the stock solution by gently lowering the jar in the vat and tipping the solution into the vat. Be careful not to let any air bubbles rise—you have just taken a lot of trouble to reduce the vat. Cover the vat and leave for 15 minutes. The vat should be yellow, perhaps with a slight touch of green. If too green, sprinkle 1 tbsp hydros over the vat, cover, and leave for a further 15 minutes.

Dyeing the Fiber, Yarn, or Fabric

1

Soak the fiber, yarn, or fabric in water in which vinegar has been added (2 tsp per 1 gal/4 l of water), letting it soak for 30 minutes. Squeeze out all excess moisture.

2

Gently immerse the fiber, yarn, or fabric into the vat and leave for 5–10 minutes. Move it about gently to make sure the indigo penetrates as evenly as possible.

3

Carefully take out the fiber, yarn, or fabric squeezing it below the surface of the dyebath and sliding it out of the vat so as not to introduce oxygen into the bath. Let it drip on the floor under some newspaper and hang to let the blue develop. If you are dyeing white fiber, it will come out of the bath a clear yellow, and quickly move toward blue; the blue will develop further over the next few minutes. If you want darker shades, the fiber can be dipped any number of times, but always let the color develop between dippings. Leave the dyed sample for a good hour or so after the last dip. Wash in mild soapy water until the water runs clear. It is best not to allow the dyed sample to dry before washing it as, once dry then washed and dried, there is the possibility of the dye rubbing off.

CORRECTING THE VAT

During the dipping process the vat may turn cloudy. Once you have taken out the fiber, yarn, or fabric, sprinkle a pinch of caustic soda on top and gently stir. If the vat becomes too green, once you have taken out the fiber, yarn, or fabric, sprinkle a pinch or two of hydros on it and gently stir. For both proceedings, wait 5 to 10 minutes or until the bath is a clear yellow.

Once your yarn has been washed and dried, re-hank it into a neat skein.

SEE ALSO:

INDIGO, PAGES 124–127
NATURAL DYES IN CONTEXT, PAGES 18–19

Single Vat Method

This method is for dyeing large amounts of yarn or fabric and is best done in the yard. A very large aluminum or galvanized metal vessel, like a garbage can, is necessary. Place the vessel on two or three bricks and light a small fire underneath to heat the water.

INGREDIENTS

- *18 oz (500 g) table salt*
- *detergent*
- *3½ oz (100 g) caustic soda*
- *9 oz (250 g) indigo powder*
- *10½ oz (300 g) hydros*

Preparing the Vat: Method

1 Fill the vessel with 17½ gal (70 l) of water and heat to no more than 120°F (49°C).

2 Add about 18 oz (500 g) of ordinary table salt and stir thoroughly. Add two or three squirts of detergent and stir gently.

3 Add 3½ oz (100 g) caustic soda and stir gently until it is dissolved. Use a long stick or broom handle that reaches to the bottom of the vessel so you can tell when the caustic soda is dissolved (the stick or broom handle will move smoothly along the bottom of the vessel).

4 Sprinkle on top 9 oz (250 g) indigo powder and stir gently. Alternatively, add the indigo to a small amount of warm water in a jar and stir until you have a smooth paste about the consistency of Ketchup. Carefully tip the paste into the vat while stirring.

5 Sprinkle 10½ oz (300 g) of hydros on top and gently stir, making sure you do not create any bubbles. Cover the vat to keep it warm. If your fire is out, wrap some old towels around the vat. Leave for a few hours, then check to see if your solution is a clear yellow. Remember, a blue sheen on top is caused by the solution's contact with air. Gently stir to see what the color of the vat is. If it is too green, sprinkle a little hydros on the top, stir, cover, and leave for a further hour.

Dyeing Techniques
Top Dyeing for Yarn

TOP DYEING (SOMETIMES CALLED BOTTOMING) MEANS DYEING ONE COLOR ON TOP OF ANOTHER. THIS IS GENERALLY DONE TO CREATE GREENS, AS TRUE GREENS ARE DIFFICULT TO GET FROM PLANT DYES, BUT THE METHOD ALSO PRODUCES DISTINCTIVE PURPLES AND LAVENDERS AND BROWNS AND BLACK.

Think in terms of painting. The method is best done by dyeing the fiber with yellow, red, orange, or purple, and then with indigo. It can be done the other way around, but you have more control of the resulting color if you dye the fiber with the base color first because indigo dips can be very short, making it possible to determine the depth of color you require.

Weld Top-dyed with Indigo

This sample was first dyed with weld, using alum-mordanted yarn. (See pages 88–89 for the recipe.) Once the yarn was dyed, it was washed and rinsed thoroughly, the hank squeezed to get rid of excess water, and then placed into an indigo bath for three minutes only. When the color has developed, you can dip it into the indigo vat again to get a darker, bluer tone.

Tansy Top-dyed with Indigo

Dyed with fresh tansy to give a good clear yellow on alum-mordanted yarn, the yarn was then washed and rinsed thoroughly and excess water squeezed from the hank. It was carefully submerged in an indigo bath for five minutes, the hank moved gently around to get an even color. Once taken from the vat and the color developed, it can be replaced in the vat for a further minute or two, but the green will become much bluer.

Meadowsweet Top-dyed with Indigo

Dyed with dried meadowsweet and a pinch of tin on alum-mordanted yarn, the yarn was washed and rinsed thoroughly and excess water squeezed out. To get the variations within the skein it was bundled loosely into a hank, submerged in the indigo vat for only half a minute, then taken out and re-bundled, and placed in the vat for a further minute. The process can be repeated, but your colors may well blend into a blue-green without the distinct variations.

Dyeing Techniques
Tie-dyeing Yarn

THERE ARE TWO METHODS OF TIE-DYEING SKEINED YARNS. ONE IS EASY AND PRODUCES RANDOM PATTERNS. THE OTHER, CALLED "SIMPLIFIED IKAT," IS DIFFICULT AND TAKES PATIENCE AND PERSEVERANCE, BUT CAN PRODUCE A REASONABLY EXACT PATTERN. INSTRUCTIONS FOR BOTH METHODS ARE BELOW AND OVER THE PAGE.

For both methods, you will need either plastic raffia (used for gardening) or plastic bags cut into thin strips for binding. For the Simplified Ikat method, you will also need two boards and two thin rods to make the skeins.

When dyeing the yarn take note of how much skein you have bound, as this will affect the amount of dye and mordant you will need. If, for example, you have bound up half the skein, then you will need 50 percent less dyestuff and mordant.

The Easy Method
This is the simplest way of getting color variations within your skein. You can start with a white skein, tie it in one or two places, and once dyed get a stark contrast between the white and the dyed. Or you can start with a dyed skein—say a cochineal color—tie it and then place it in an indigo vat for a red or purple-pink effect. Once knitted or woven, the result will either be bold (if you started with a white skein) or muted (if you started with a dyed skein).

1

The skeins should be thin, as this will make the binding easier to control, and short, if you are only going to tie, or bind, in one place. Make them longer if you want to bind in more than one place. Take the area you want to bind between thumb and finger, squeeze, and wind the plastic tightly around that area, making sure there are no gaps. Go around once or twice, then tie the two ends together. Choose the dye recipe to make sure there will be contrast between the dyed and undyed colors. Follow the dyeing instructions of your chosen recipe (see pages 88–129).

2

When the dyeing is complete and the yarn has been washed, undo the bindings.

3

You can now lay the skein out and rebind it in a different place, or places, perhaps covering most of the dyed color, and dye with another color. Indigo is the easiest.

This skein was mordanted with alum, dyed with madder, washed, re-bound and dyed with cochineal, washed, bound once more, and dipped in an indigo vat for three minutes to create an harmonious color scheme.

Experiment with different mordants to create a subtle range of analogous colors, all within the same yarn ball. This skein was pre-mordanted and bound, dyed with madder, then re-bound and replaced in the madder bath with a pinch of tin.

If tie-dyeing with just one color on white yarn, you will get a sharp color contrast, but also a slight bleeding of the color into the white, which gives a great effect. The sample skein was mordanted with alum then tied and dyed with cochineal.

You can tie and dye as many times as you wish, in as many different baths as you wish, but it is best not to go over three or four, or the colors will begin to muddy.

To create subtle gradations of the same color within the same skein, use one dye bath—in this case, indigo—but dip for different lengths of time with every tie you do.

This skein was pre-mordanted with alum, bound and dyed with logwood, then re-bound. A pinch of iron was stirred into the exhaust bath and the re-bound hank re-entered and simmered for half an hour.

▶ **SEE ALSO:**
TIE-DYEING TEXTILES, PAGES 78–79
ALL ABOUT COLOR, PAGES 36–41

Simplified Ikat

The patterning with ikat is more exact and can only be done with skeins of equal length. To prepare the skein it is essential that you know the exact length of each row to be knitted or woven. This method works best for items of narrow width.

1

Knit or weave a sample piece in the width you wish the finished piece to be. Mark the beginning just before your first cast-on stitch for knitting, or use a piece of tied yarn to mark the beginning of your weaving. Knit or weave eight rows, marking the beginning and end of each row.

2

Undo your work and measure the length of each row. The rows should be the same or very close to the same. Even tension when knitting is difficult but essential. With weaving it is easier. The average length of your rows will be the length of your skeins. However, if the length is too long, then divide the length of the row in half or quarters and make the skein accordingly. In other words, the distance from one end of the skein to the other will either be half or a quarter of the row.

3

To make the skeins the proper size you will have to make a skein holder. For this, you will need two boards about 3 in (8 cm) longer than the required length of your skein. You will also need two dowel rods of equal length, at least half the size of your boards. Drill holes at either end of your boards, which will hold the rods. The holes should be the same distance from each other as the length of your skein. For example, if your rows averaged 10 in (25 cm), the skein is 10 in (25 cm) in length; the holes will be set at the same distance—i.e, 10 in (25 cm). If your row averaged 30 in (76 cm), and you have folded it in half, the distance between the holes will be 15 in (38 cm). If your row averaged 80 in (200 cm), and you have folded the skein in half twice, then the distance between the holes will be 20 in (50 cm).

4

Now place your rods into the holes and then place your other board, which also has holes drilled at the proper distance, on top of your rods to hold them upright. This is to keep them from bending inward when you are winding your skein around the rods.

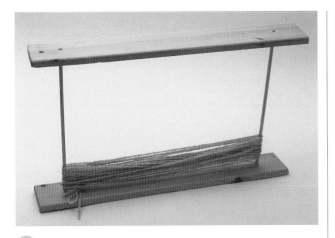

5

Wind the skein carefully around the rods, leaving a 2 or 3 in (5 or 8 cm) length for tying up the skein, and making sure you wind them around the rods evenly, starting at the very bottom and working your way up round by round so that each round is of the same length. Finish at the same side you began so that you can tie the two ends together.

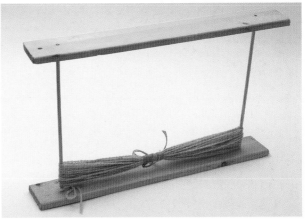

6

Without removing the skein, bind the area or areas you wish not to take up the dye with the plastic. Bind carefully so as not to leave any gaps. Wind the binding material around the area two or three times, then tie the two ends together. Take the top board off the skein holder.

8

Once washed, remove the bindings and dry the skein. It is then ready to be knitted or woven. You should have a clearly delineated pattern but if not try again. Once you have mastered the procedure, you can attempt more complicated designs by retying and redyeing the skein.

7

Carefully remove the skein and follow the dyeing instructions for the "Easy Method" (see pages 66–67). For your first try, indigo is the easiest, which is what has been used for the example.

SEE ALSO:

SKEINING YARN, PAGE 28

Dyeing Techniques
Random Dyeing for Yarn

IN TIE-DYEING THE SEPARATION OF COLORS IS DISTINCT WHEREAS IN THESE RANDOM METHODS, THE COLORS CAN BLEND ONE INTO ANOTHER. AS A RESULT, IT IS IMPORTANT TO DYE WITH COLORS THAT COMPLEMENT ONE ANOTHER RATHER THAN CONTRAST AND TO DYE WITH RECIPES USING THE SAME MORDANT, AS YOU CAN ONLY MORDANT YOUR FIBER ONCE. SO CHOOSE YOUR RECIPES CAREFULLY.

Knotting process   Two-shade process   Two-color process   Four-color process

Experiment with different mordants to create a two-shade skein, or prepare two different dye vats to dye your yarn in complementary colors.

NOTE

For the two-shade, two- and four-color processes, wooden rods are necessary. Rest the rod on top of the dyebath with half of the skein draped over it so that half of it is out of the water. You may have to adjust the amount of water in the dyebath to accommodate this process.

Knotting Process

1

For this method, the longer the skeins the better. Simply knot the skeins in two or three places; the knots should be as tight as possible. The inside of the knot should remain white after dyeing, but there will be some bleeding of the dyestuff into the outer surfaces of the knots.

2

Dye the skeins in one color; untie the knots and tie another series. If you do not want white in your skein, make sure you knot only over the previously dyed parts of the skein. If you wish to have white in the skein, then tie knots over some or all of the white from your first dyeing.

3

Dye the skeins in a complementary color. Undo the knots and you should have at least three colors, four if you choose to leave some of your areas white.

Two-shade Process

Mordant half your skein with one mordant and the other half with another. Alum and copper work well. Now dye your skein in one dyebath to produce two subtle colors, with a slight blending of the two where they meet.

This yarn was dyed with madder using the two-shade process. Half the skein was mordanted with alum, the other half with copper.

Two-color Process

Mordant your skein with one mordant, then dye half in one color, and the other half in another. However, make sure the colors you choose will blend well where they meet.

This skein was first mordanted with alum, then half dyed in cochineal and the other half in logwood.

Four-color Process

Mordant half the skein with one mordant, the other half with another. Now arrange the skein so that half contains both mordants. Dye this half in one dyebath, which will allow two colors to be produced. Dye the other half in a different dyebath. This skein will have four colors.

In this example, half the skein was mordanted with alum, to which a pinch of tin had been added, the other half with copper, to which a pinch of tin was also added. The skein was then dyed with cochineal and logwood.

▶ **SEE ALSO:**

MULTICOLOR DYEING FOR TEXTILES, PAGES 76–77

Dyeing Techniques
Expanded Dyeing for Yarn

LET'S ASSUME YOU HAVE NOW DONE YOUR FIRST DYEINGS WITH COCHINEAL, MADDER, LOGWOOD, AND YELLOWS. WITH THE EXCEPTION OF THE YELLOW EXHAUST BATH, YOU WILL NOTE THAT THERE IS STILL A LOT OF COLOR SUSPENDED IN THE OTHER POTS. JUST MAKE SURE, WHEN TAKING THE FIBER OUT OF THE DYEBATH, THAT YOU SQUEEZE IT THOROUGHLY, LETTING THE SQUEEZED WATER DRIP BACK INTO THE DYEPOT TO CONSERVE AS MUCH OF THE EXHAUST AS POSSIBLE.

You might as well empty the yellow exhaust pot, but the material you boiled can be saved. Add onionskins—a good handful for every 3½ oz (100 g) of plant boiled—and boil it again. The liquor from this boiling, with copper-mordanted fiber, will produce a greenish yellow or a mustard yellow, depending on the original dyeplant.

The various combinations to use with your exhaust baths are shown below. The important thing is to experiment: with dyestuffs, with combinations, and above all with enthusiasm and imagination! After all, if something goes wrong and you don't like the resulting color, you can put the offending fiber into an indigo bath. You'll get something approaching a brown or black or perhaps a khaki-blue color. It depends, of course, on what color you put into the indigo. So don't be put off.

The samples below show that the original dyebaths all used alum-mordanted fiber. If you have used copper or altered the color with tin or iron, the resultant colors will be very different.

Cochineal (see pages 100–101 for original recipe)

Add powdered madder (1¾ oz/50 g per 3½ oz/100 g of yarn) and your copper-mordanted fiber for a deep brown-red.

Add onionskins (a good handful per 3½ oz/100 g of yarn) a pinch of tin, and your alum-mordanted fiber for a bright orange-red.

Use alum-mordanted fiber for a dark pink (but lightfastness will not be quite as good as in the original recipe).

Use an alum-mordanted fiber as before but then overdye with indigo for a lovely purple-pink.

Madder (see pages 98–99 for original recipe)

Add cochineal (about 1 oz/30 g per 3½ oz/100 g of yarn) and your copper-mordanted fiber for dark brick red.

Add cochineal and alum-mordanted fiber for a light brick red.

Add onionskins (a good handful per 1¾ oz/100 g of yarn) and copper-mordanted fiber for a light orange-brown.

Logwood (see pages 104–105 for original recipe)

Add a second boiling of logwood chips and then add copper-mordanted yarn for a blue-purple.

Add onionskins (1¾ oz/50 g per 3½ oz/100 g of yarn) and copper-mordanted fiber for a blue-green.

Add cochineal (1 oz/30 g per 3½ oz/100 g of yarn) and copper-mordanted yarn for a deep blue-purple.

Dyeing Techniques
Dyeing Fabric: An Introduction

DYEING TEXTILES WITH NATURAL DYES IS AN INTERESTING MIXTURE OF BEING EXACTLY THE SAME AS DYEING YARNS WITH NATURAL DYES AND TOTALLY DIFFERENT. WHILE ON THE SURFACE THE TWO SHOULD BE VERY SIMILAR (AFTER ALL, IT IS WOOL YARN THAT MAKES WOOL FABRIC), THE PROCESS OF MAKING FABRIC— EITHER BY WEAVING OR KNITTING—AND THE PHYSICALITY OF HANDLING FABRIC IN A DYEBATH MAKE IT VERY DIFFERENT.

Turmeric produces a good orange-yellow color as the powder suggests, but it is not a fast permanent color.

Preparing for Dyeing

Bought yarn is always labeled with the yarn content; bought fabric is often not labeled with the exact makeup of the fabric. It is quite common, for example, to see a synthetic fabric labeled as silk when, in fact, it only has a very small silk content or just a silklike finish. When fabrics are made into clothes, they are then correctly labeled. However, you need to read the label carefully, paying attention to the proportion of the fabric types used to make up a particular cloth. If you are in any doubt about the fabric content or want to know whether the fabric is a natural fiber or not, it can be worth doing a burn test to check the fiber content (see table below). Now measure the amount of fabric that you need to make the project but do not neglect the scouring (see pages 34–35) and mordanting (see page 59) stages, as the best results are always obtained when the best preparation is observed.

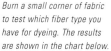
Burn a small corner of fabric to test which fiber type you have for dyeing. The results are shown in the chart below.

Fabric	Burns or Melts	Flame	Smoke Color	Speed	Smell	Crumble Factor
Cotton	Burns	Yellow	Gray	Fast	Burning paper	Soft, gray, feathery fine ash
Linen	Burns	Yellow	Gray	Fast	Burning paper	Soft, gray, feathery fine ash
Silk	Burns	Irregular	Gray	Slow	Burning hair or feathers	Easily crushable ash, brittle
Wool	Burns	Irregular	Gray	Slow	Burning hair or feathers	Easily crushable ash, brittle

Basic Dyeing Method

Choose a recipe from pages 106–129, and follow the steps below. The method is demonstrated here with turmeric.

① Place the dye in an old thin sock or leg from a panty hose. Following the recipe of your choice, raise the temperature slowly in the dyepot. Stir the dye-powder sock around the pan to ensure all the color is released.

② Carefully place your fabric into the dyepot. The water will be extremely hot, so use a stirring stick or rod to push the fabric fully under the dye waterline.

③ Check how the fabric is taking the dye color by using the stirring rod to remove it from the dyepot. If it is not the required color, replace it and/or add more dyestuff.

④ Once you have the correct color, you can use the stirring stick or rod to remove the fabric from the dyepot and into a bowl that can then be easily taken to the sink for washing and rinsing.

DYEING EVENLY

Make sure you spread out your fabric in the dyepot. All of the fabric must be under the water at all times. If any fabric is above the water, which can often happen when the fabric gets air bubbles, this out-of-water section will not be dyeing at the same rate as the rest, which means that you are more likely to end up with a patchily dyed fabric.

Dyeing Techniques
Multicolor Dyeing for Textiles

WHILE OFTEN TRICKY TO ACHIEVE AT FIRST, THIS IS A TECHNIQUE THAT CAN GIVE BEAUTIFUL RESULTS. PLAN AHEAD AND HAVE ALL INGREDIENTS AND DYEPOTS READY SO THAT YOU CAN WORK BACKWARD AND FORWARD BETWEEN THE COLORS YOU WISH TO USE.

There are numerous methods that can be used to dye fabrics a mixture of colors:

• Dye half of your fabric in one dyebath, rinse it through, and then dye the other end in a dyebath of another color to give a two-color fabric.

• To achieve a gradation of color, start the fabric in a weak dyebath. Add more dye in regular increments and, at the same time, remove sections of the fabric from the dyebath. The weakest color will have had the least time and dye, while the strongest will have had the longest time and amount of color.

The strongest end of a gradated fabric can then be added to a dyebath of another color to tilt it in a different color direction from the rest of the fabric.

• Resist methods such as tie-dyeing, clamping, and batik are generally the most common way to achieve a mixture of colors on fabrics. Dip a white or unbleached fabric into a dyebath and then rinse. Either remove all the resist and dip into another dyebath or add more resist and then dip into another dyebath. The second option can be repeated several times in different colors by adding layers of color.

The Method

1 Place half of the fabric into a plastic bag to keep it clean. Carefully place the rest of the fabric into the dyepot. You will need to hold the covered fabric out of the water, which will be extremely hot, and push the fabric that is in the dyepot under the waterline and stir.

2 When you have achieved your first color, remove the fabric from the dyepot and rinse this end of fabric under cold running water.

Mix whatever colors you want on the fabric; they can be contrasting or complementary colors.

▶ SEE ALSO:
RANDOM DYEING FOR YARN, PAGES 70–71

3 Place the dyed end of fabric into a plastic bag and repeat Step 1 in your second color dyepot or if you are changing the tone of color, only place the fabric back into your original dyepot until you have the second color that you want.

4 Rinse the fabric well under cold running water until all the excess dye color has been removed. Wring out by hand to remove any excess water.

OVERDYEING TEXTILES

When used on their own, natural dyes can give some of the most beautiful colors on fabrics, but if you overdye (using more than one color on one piece of fabric), you can open up a whole new range of colors and tones for your fabrics.

Ancient and Modern Dyeing Techniques

Nearly all the colors that you see and use today are made from more than one original color pot. Often two or three colors make up the tone and strength of color for any one item. However, if you look at old fabrics, they often seem dull with a very limited range of colors. This is because some of the natural dyes used when they were made may well have been fugitive, not able to withstand the light or not washfast to any degree. And the colors that have survived the test of time may once have been brighter, stronger, deeper, or even a completely different color altogether.

Making Green and Orange

There are some colors, such as green, that are not readily available which is surprising considering all the plant material used in natural dyes. Green leaves and shoots usually give yellow to brown tones. But use those plants to get the yellow color and then dip them into indigo and you have green; dip them into cochineal and you have orange.

Subtle Changes

You don't have to make such big changes in color when overdyeing; you can use a weak solution of dye to make the original color warmer or colder, dirtier or fresher looking. Often with natural dyes, you start your fabric in a dyebath that is running out of strength of color, so your first coloring is weak. But then you add the fabric to a second stronger bath of another dye color and the result is a new color.

Overdyeing Colored or Patterned Fabric

You can buy fabrics that already has a color or a pattern and overdye them. Bought fabrics will usually have been dyed with a synthetic commercial dye but, as long as the fabric is 100 percent natural, you can prepare it in the usual way with a scouring (see pages 34–35) and mordant (see page 59) treatment, and then overdye with a natural dye of your choice. This is a really good way to pep up old fabrics around the house or in your wardrobe, making them fresh and new again for use a second time around.

Dyeing Techniques
Tie-dyeing Textiles

TIE-DYE WORKS AS A RESIST METHOD OF PATTERNING FABRICS. OFTEN REFERRED TO AS SHIBORI, FROM THE JAPANESE METHOD OF WORKING, THIS WAY OF PATTERNING FABRICS HAS BEEN USED FOR CENTURIES AND ACROSS DIFFERENT CONTINENTS.

Tie-dye is still used today, with each region passing down its own traditions, patterns, techniques, and tools. Some use the finest threads, stitching intricate patterns into the cloth to form the resist for the dye. Others use small stones or pips tied into the fabric to make patterns. Some pleat the fabric around poles or use leather strips to tie the fabric.

Tie-dye Methods

Fabric is bound, pleated, or stitched with thread and then immersed into a dyebath. The color can only penetrate or attach itself where there is no thread, leaving these areas clear. It can take days or weeks to stitch or tie some of the more intricate patterns that you can see in museums or on Japanese kimonos. These fabrics are also dipped over numerous stages. However, beginners can create simple patterns such as stripes and circles at home in a great deal less time!

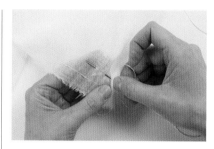

Running Stitch

A simple running stitch can be pulled tightly to form a stitched resist pattern. This can be random or planned out on the fabric beforehand. Use tailor's chalk to get evenly spaced lines and stitches.

Twisted

Twisted fabric is wrapped around a piece of wood, in this case an old coat hanger, and tied tightly to the wood to keep it in a twisted form when it goes into the dyebath.

Resist Pattern

Fabric can be stitched and then twisted around a pole or wooden length to form a resist pattern. You can also twist the fabric into a pattern without stitching beforehand.

Pattern of Lines

You can tie-dye fabric pieces or lengths or even readymade garments. This 100% cotton undershirt has a few elastic bands tightly binding the middle section to form a simple pattern of lines.

Pieces of tied fabric ready to be tie-dyed.

▶ **SEE ALSO:**

TIE-DYEING YARN, PAGES 66–69

The Method

1 Carefully place your tied fabric or garment into the dyepot. The water will be extremely hot so use a stirring stick or rod to push the fabric fully under the dye waterline. Leave in the dyepot until the required color is achieved.

2 Carefully remove from the dyepot and rinse the fabric well under cold running water until all the excess dye color has been removed. Wring out by hand to remove any excess water.

3 Cut away all the ties so that you can start to see the tie-dye pattern you have created. The ties are very tight to the fabric so take great care not to cut the fabric or garment.

4 After rinsing in cold running water, wash the fabric for a short time in a bowl of warm water with a small amount of pH-neutral washing powder.

Dyeing Techniques
Resist Dyeing Fabrics with Indigo

INDIGO IS OFTEN USED AS THE NATURAL DYE FOR RESIST METHODS
OF PATTERNING FABRICS. BECAUSE THE DYE IS USED AT A LOWER
TEMPERATURE THAN MOST OTHER NATURAL DYE COLORS, YOU CAN
RESIST WITH A WIDER RANGE OF TECHNIQUES USING THIS DYE.

All of the tie-dyeing (pages 78–79) and batik (pages 84–85) techniques available can use indigo as the natural dye but you can also make other designs of resist by clamping the fabric between boards or wooden shapes. These can be either plain or have a pattern engraved onto two symmetrical blocks, which

will then transfer to the fabric when it is clamped between them.

As indigo is a natural dye that has been used for centuries around the world, the methods of patterning using this dye have a long history, each region with its own design patterns and techniques that it uses.

You can easily dye at home using simple shapes of wood, ceramic tiles, or metal shapes and woodworkers' clamps to hold the fabric in place. Sometimes old blocks or reproduction blocks can be bought at flea markets or online for you to experiment with.

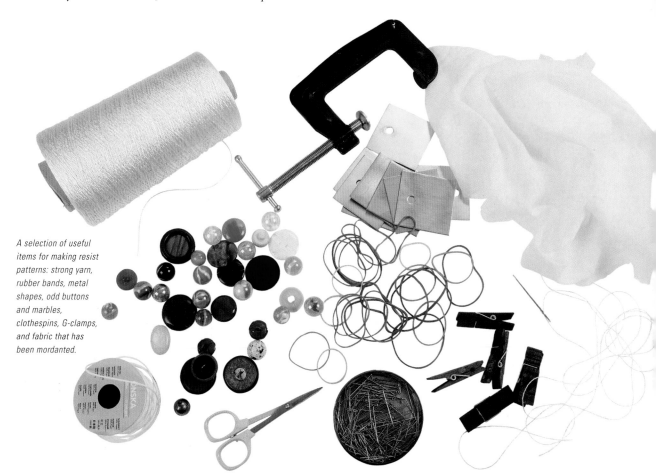

A selection of useful items for making resist patterns: strong yarn, rubber bands, metal shapes, odd buttons and marbles, clothespins, G-clamps, and fabric that has been mordanted.

Method Variations

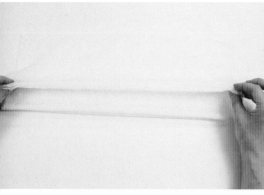 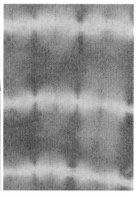

Folding

You can fold fabric before you clamp it to add another pattern element to the design.

The folds can be as simple or as complex as you want. This simple fold is made to match the square shape of the metal pieces for clamping.

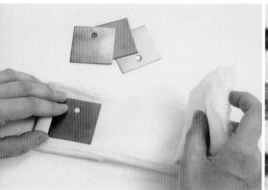 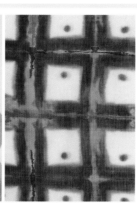

Clamping (see page 83)

You can insert the metal pieces while folding, or you can fold the fabric into a small square and then place a metal resist piece at the back and front of the folded fabric. When the fabric is folded with the metal pieces in place, position the G-clamp on the metal and screw tightly, pushing the metal plates together to form a resist that the dye cannot penetrate.

Marbles (see page 82)

Children's marbles and string can be used to make a resist pattern. You can also use seeds that have been baked hard in an oven or small stones instead of the marbles. When tying the marbles into the fabric you can make a random pattern or plan a design beforehand, marking the fabric with tailor's chalk to show where to tie the marbles. Place the marble in the fabric.

Pegs

Experiment with different household objects such as clothes-pegs. Different styles of pegs will leave different resist patterns to create a wide range of designs.

You can use the marble-tying technique with lots of different recipes to make the fabrics a wide range of colors.

Using Marbles

The Method

When placing the fabric in the bath make sure to keep it as open and spread out as possible. Replace the lid as quickly as you can to stop the bath deteriorating. Follow the recipes on pages 124–127 for dipping and oxidizing lengths of time in the indigo vat.

Make sure that you have a bowl, bucket, or tray ready to catch any drips as you remove the fabric from the indigo bath. Squeezing too much excess indigo liquid from the fabric back into the indigo bath can cause air bubbles in the bath. Replace the lid on the indigo bath as soon as possible to keep the indigo fresh.

An old clotheshorse or a washline can be used to oxidize the fabric. Make sure that the fabric is spread out so that as much of the surface as possible can be oxidized by the air. Rinse the fabric well under cold running water until all the excess dye color has been removed. Wring out by hand to remove any excess water.

Cut away all the ties so that you can start to see the tie-dye pattern you have created. The ties are very tight to the fabric so take great care not to cut the fabric or garment.

Using Clamps

The Method

2

Remove the clamped fabric from the indigo bath and let it drip over a bowl to remove some of the excess indigo dye. An old clotheshorse or a washline can be used to oxidize the fabric. Make sure that the fabric is spread out so that as much of the surface as possible can be oxidized by the air.

1

Fold the fabric piece into pleats and place small metal flat plates at regular intervals down the length of the pleated fabric. Fold this into small squares trapping the metal plates. Place this folded fabric into a G-clamp and tighten to hold all the fabric and metal plates in place.

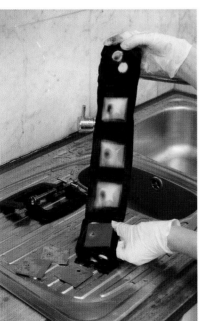

3

Rinse the fabric while it's still in the clamp to remove any excess dye. Remove the clamp, taking care not to damage the wet fabric with the metal resist pieces.

4

Rinse the fabric well under cold running water until all the excess dye color has been removed. Wring out by hand to remove any excess water.

The square metal plates leave a square pattern on the fabric while the G-clamp leaves spots.

▶ SEE ALSO:
NATURAL DYES IN CONTEXT, PAGES 18–19
INDIGO, PAGES 124–127

Dyeing Techniques
Batik Dyeing for Textiles

EXAMPLES OF BATIK-PATTERNED FABRICS FROM ASIA, INDIA, AND AFRICA DATE BACK 2,000 YEARS. THE WORD "BATIK" IS THOUGHT TO COME FROM THE MALAY WORD MEANING "TO WRITE" OR "TO DOT."

Early examples from Indonesia, one of the main batik-dyeing areas, indicate that this was an activity for the women of the royal court. The patterns have been passed down over the centuries; individual patterns often have an underlying meaning for the wearer such as good luck, prosperity, or health.

Batik fabrics are patterned by applying a design of hot melted wax to the fabric. The waxed fabric is then dyed, the wax forming a resist to the dye. The wax is removed by applying heat; the undyed area forms the design. There are many batik kits available for the home dyer. However, as the main design element is a dot of wax, it is quite simple, after a little practice, to pattern your own fabric without a kit. The dye used by natural dyers for batik patterns is usually indigo. You cannot use a hot dye as it will melt the wax, but you can achieve tones of color by waxing and dipping in stages as you add to the design.

If you don't have a specialized wax pot for batik patterning you can use a bain-marie (or double-boiler system) for melting the wax, but it must be in old pans that will not be used for cooking.

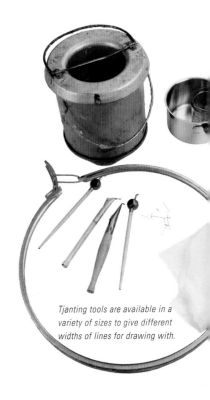

Tjanting tools are available in a variety of sizes to give different widths of lines for drawing with.

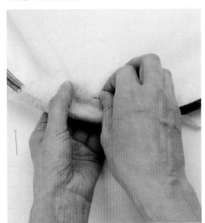

Batik wax can be applied to form spots as well as lines. By repeating the application of wax you can cover larger areas with the wax resist.

The Method

1

The fabric needs to be stretched over a frame. This can be a specialized batik or silk-painting frame or you can find your own frames to use. The fabric can be lightly pinned (as shown here), or stretched tightly across the frame for more complex designs.

2

Using melted hot wax and a tjanting tool, quickly draw your pattern onto the fabric. Hold the wax pot close to the fabric so that the hot wax does not have time to cool, which makes it harder to draw. You can draw a simple spot pattern or lines, or you can use your own photographs or nature for inspiration. It is a good idea to practice with the tjanting tool on some scrap fabric before working on a final piece.

3

Dip the fabric in an indigo dyebath. Note that the wax design shows as a paler color against the indigo. When oxidizing, spread out the fabric or garment as much as possible so that the nonwaxed fabric can fully develop its indigo color.

4

You can dip and oxidize the fabric several times to increase the depth of blue and the contrast between the waxed and nonwaxed areas. Leave the batik fabric to oxidize on a clotheshorse.

HISTORY OF BATIK PATTERNING

In Central African countries it is common for the resist to be a cassava or rice paste instead of hot wax. It can take days or weeks to wax-pattern the fabrics, depending on the complexity of the pattern and the number of color layers, each of which will require protection under a layer of wax or paste. When carved pattern blocks were introduced, the dyer was able to apply the wax or resist paste more quickly to cover more area, but it is patterns made with handtools—which have changed little over the centuries—that are most admired today.

Use nature to inspire a free handdrawn design onto a children's T-shirt.

▶ **SEE ALSO:**
NATURAL DYES IN CONTEXT, PAGES 18–19
INDIGO, PAGES 124–127

Recipes

Recipes for dyeing fabrics and yarns are very similar to cooking recipes. They vary from country to country depending on the availability of ingredients and the local traditions and they are handed down through families or businesses, often a much-guarded secret. While some core ingredients need to stay in the recipe, much like cooking, other details can easily be changed to achieve different colors or tones on a wide range of fabrics and yarns.

Recipes

Weld

(Reseda luteola)

WELD IS ALSO KNOWN AS DYER'S WEED, DYER'S ROCKET, AND DYER'S MIGNONETTE. UNLIKE OTHER FLOWERING PLANTS USED FOR NATURAL DYEING, THE DYE IS CONCENTRATED IN ITS SEEDS RATHER THAN IN THE FLOWERS.

General Method

1 Place the weld in cold water and slowly bring to the boil.
2 Boil for 30 minutes.
3 When cool, strain into the dyepot, place the yarn in the dyebath, add enough water to cover the yarn, and bring slowly to just under boiling point.
4 Boil for 30 minutes or until the desired color is reached.
5 When cool enough to handle—do not leave in the dyebath longer than is necessary—wash the yarn with mild soapy water and then rinse until the water runs clear.

▶ SEE ALSO:
FLOWERS, PAGE 46

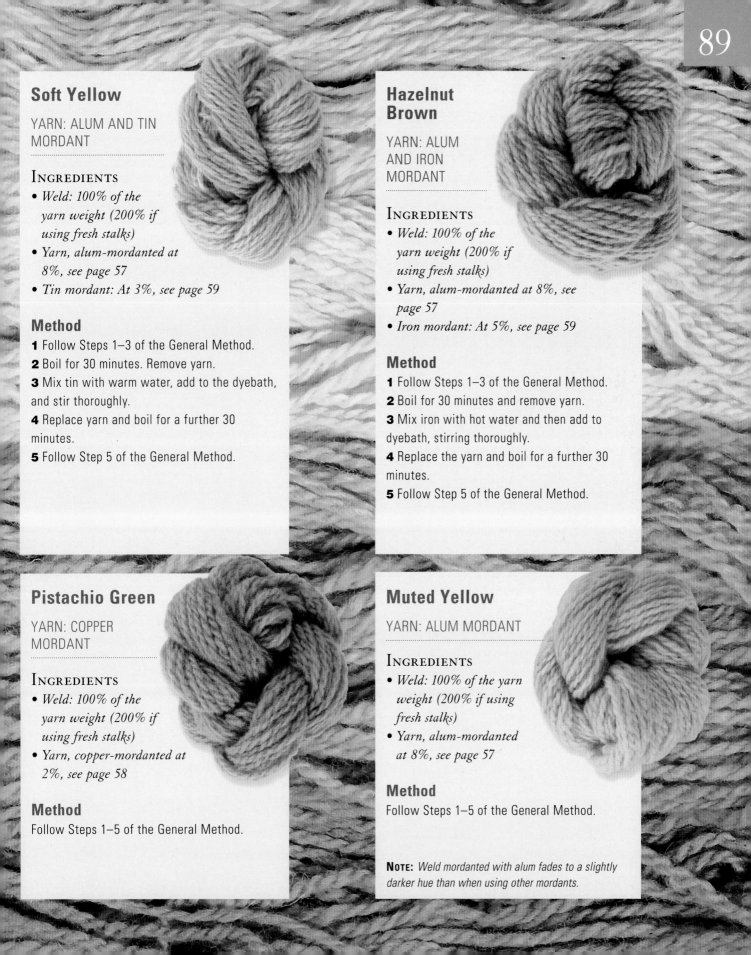

Soft Yellow

YARN: ALUM AND TIN
MORDANT

INGREDIENTS
- *Weld: 100% of the yarn weight (200% if using fresh stalks)*
- *Yarn, alum-mordanted at 8%, see page 57*
- *Tin mordant: At 3%, see page 59*

Method
1 Follow Steps 1–3 of the General Method.
2 Boil for 30 minutes. Remove yarn.
3 Mix tin with warm water, add to the dyebath, and stir thoroughly.
4 Replace yarn and boil for a further 30 minutes.
5 Follow Step 5 of the General Method.

Hazelnut Brown

YARN: ALUM
AND IRON
MORDANT

INGREDIENTS
- *Weld: 100% of the yarn weight (200% if using fresh stalks)*
- *Yarn, alum-mordanted at 8%, see page 57*
- *Iron mordant: At 5%, see page 59*

Method
1 Follow Steps 1–3 of the General Method.
2 Boil for 30 minutes and remove yarn.
3 Mix iron with hot water and then add to dyebath, stirring thoroughly.
4 Replace the yarn and boil for a further 30 minutes.
5 Follow Step 5 of the General Method.

Pistachio Green

YARN: COPPER
MORDANT

INGREDIENTS
- *Weld: 100% of the yarn weight (200% if using fresh stalks)*
- *Yarn, copper-mordanted at 2%, see page 58*

Method
Follow Steps 1–5 of the General Method.

Muted Yellow

YARN: ALUM MORDANT

INGREDIENTS
- *Weld: 100% of the yarn weight (200% if using fresh stalks)*
- *Yarn, alum-mordanted at 8%, see page 57*

Method
Follow Steps 1–5 of the General Method.

NOTE: *Weld mordanted with alum fades to a slightly darker hue than when using other mordants.*

Recipes

Goldenrod

(Solidago sp., especially Canadensis ssp.)

LIKE SO MANY PLANTS USED FOR DYEING, GOLDENROD HAS MEDICINAL USES AS A CLEANSING AGENT. IT ALSO CONTAINS RUBBER.

General Method

1 Boil flowers in plenty of water for 2 to 3 hours. Cool in the pot overnight.

2 Strain the liquor into the dyepot and place the mordanted yarn in the bath.

3 Bring slowly to just under boiling point.

4 Simmer for 60 minutes or until required depth of color is obtained.

5 When cool enough to handle, wash the yarn in mild soapy water and then rinse until the water runs clear.

▶ SEE ALSO:

FLOWERS, PAGE 46

Bright Yellow

YARN: ALUM AND
TIN MORDANT

INGREDIENTS
- *Fresh flowers:
  100% of the yarn
  weight, or*
- *Dried flowers: 50%
  of the yarn weight*
- *Yarn, alum-mordanted at 8%, see page 57*
- *Tin mordant: At 3%, see page 59*

Method
1 Follow Steps 1–3 of the General Method.
2 Simmer for 30 minutes or until required depth of color is obtained. Remove yarn.
3 Mix tin with warm water and add to dyebath, stirring well to distribute.
4 Replace the yarn and simmer for a further 30 minutes.
5 Follow Step 5 of the General Method.

Dark Olive Green

YARN: ALUM AND IRON
MORDANT

INGREDIENTS
- *Fresh flowers: 100% of the
  yarn weight, or*
- *Dried flowers: 50% of the
  yarn weight*
- *Yarn, alum-mordanted at 8%,
  see page 57*
- *Iron mordant: At 5%, see page 59*

Method
1 Follow Steps 1–3 of the General Method.
2 Simmer for 30 minutes. Remove yarn.
3 Mix iron with warm water and add to the dyebath, stirring well to distribute.
4 Replace the yarn, and simmer for a further 30 minutes.
5 Follow Step 5 of the General Method.

Rich Olive Green

YARN: COPPER
MORDANT

INGREDIENTS
- *Fresh flowers: 100%
  of the yarn weight, or*
- *Dried flowers: 50%
  of the yarn weight*
- *Yarn, copper-mordanted at
  2%, see page 58*

Method
Follow Steps 1–5 of the General Method.

Lemon Yellow

YARN: ALUM MORDANT

INGREDIENTS
- *Fresh flowers: 100% of the
  yarn weight, or*
- *Dried flowers: 50% of the
  yarn weight*
- *Yarn, alum-mordanted at 8%,
  see page 57*

Method
Follow Steps 1–5 of the General Method.

Recipes

Heather

(Calluna vulgaris)

ALTHOUGH LING (*Calluna vulgaris*) IS MOST COMMONLY USED FOR DYEING, ALL HEATHERS WILL PRODUCE SIMILAR COLORS. THESE RECIPES USE HEATHER COLLECTED IN LATE SUMMER. HEATHER FROM A SUPPLIER GAVE DULLER TONES.

General Method

1 Place the tips in cold water and slowly bring to the boil. Boil for at least 60 minutes.
2 When cool, strain into the dyepot and add the yarn. If necessary, add more water to cover the yarn completely.
3 Slowly bring to just under boiling point.
4 Simmer for about 60 minutes.
5 When cool enough to handle—do not leave the yarn in the dyebath any longer than is necessary—take out the yarn, wash it in mild soapy water, and then rinse until the water runs clear.

▶ SEE ALSO:

FLOWERS, PAGE 46

Buttermilk Yellow

YARN: ALUM MORDANT

INGREDIENTS
- *Fresh heather tips: 100% of the yarn weight, or*
- *Dried tips: 50% of the yarn weight*
- *Yarn, alum-mordanted at 8%, see page 57*

Method
Follow Steps 1–5 of the General Method.

Bright Yellow

YARN: ALUM AND TIN MORDANT

INGREDIENTS
- *Fresh heather tips: 100% of the yarn weight, or*
- *Dried tips: 50% of the yarn weight*
- *Yarn, alum-mordanted at 8%, see page 57*
- *Tin mordant: At 3%, see page 59*

Method
1 Follow Steps 1–3 of the General Method.
2 Simmer for about 30 minutes. Remove yarn.
3 Dissolve the tin in warm water and add to the dyebath, mixing thoroughly.
4 Replace the yarn and simmer for a further 30 minutes.
5 Follow Step 5 of the General Method.

Golden Olive

YARN: COPPER
MORDANT

INGREDIENTS
- *Fresh heather tips: 100% of the yarn weight, or*
- *Dried tips: 50% of the yarn weight*
- *Yarn, copper-mordanted at 2%, see page 58*

Method
Follow Steps 1–5 of the General Method.

Slate Olive

YARN: ALUM AND
IRON MORDANT

INGREDIENTS
- *Fresh heather tips: 100% of the yarn weight, or*
- *Dried tips: 50% of the yarn weight*
- *Yarn, alum-mordanted at 8%, see page 57*
- *Iron mordant: At 5%, see page 59*

Method
1 Follow Steps 1–3 of the General Method.
2 Simmer for about 30 minutes. Remove yarn.
3 Dissolve the iron in warm water and add to the dyebath, stirring well.
4 Replace the yarn and simmer for a further 30 minutes.
5 Follow Step 5 of the General Method.

Recipes

Elder

(Sambucus nigra and canadensis)

The berries can be used for dyeing, but the colors fade quickly. Although older leaves can be used, the best colors are derived from fresh young leaves collected in late spring.

General Method

1 Place the leaves in a saucepan with enough water to cover. Bring slowly up to the boil and boil for at least 30 minutes. If you boil for too long, the color may brown.

2 When cold, strain into your dyepot. Add your yarn and more water if necessary.

3 Bring slowly up to just under the boil.

4 Simmer for 60 minutes.

5 When cool enough to handle, wash in warm soapy water and then rinse until the water runs clear.

▶SEE ALSO:
LEAVES, PAGE 48
BERRIES, PAGE 53

Pale Moss Green

YARN: COPPER AND IRON MORDANT

INGREDIENTS
- *Young leaves: 200% of the yarn weight*
- *Yarn, copper-mordanted at 2%, see page 58*
- *Iron mordant: At 5%, see page 59*

Method
1 Follow Steps 1–3 of the General Method.
2 Simmer for 30 minutes.
3 Lift out the yarn and add the iron, mixed with some hot water, and stir thoroughly.
4 Replace the yarn and simmer for a further 30 minutes.
5 Follow Step 5 of the General Method.

Bright Yellow

YARN: ALUM AND TIN MORDANT

INGREDIENTS
- *Fresh leaves: 200% of the yarn weight*
- *Yarn, alum-mordanted at 8%, see page 57*
- *Tin mordant: At 3%, see page 59*

Method
1 Follow Steps 1–3 of the General Method.
2 Simmer for 30 minutes.
3 Lift out the yarn and add the tin, mixed with some warm water, to the dyebath, and stir thoroughly.
4 Replace the yarn and simmer for a further 30 minutes.
5 Follow Step 5 of the General Method.

Mustard Yellow

YARN: COPPER MORDANT

INGREDIENTS
- *Young leaves: 200% of the yarn weight*
- *Yarn, copper-mordanted at 2%, see page 58*

Method
1 Follow Steps 1–3 of the General Method.
2 Simmer for 30 minutes or until desired color is obtained.
3 Follow Step 5 of the General Method.

Clear Yellow

YARN: ALUM MORDANT

INGREDIENTS
- *Fresh leaves: 200% of the yarn weight*
- *Yarn, alum-mordanted at 8%, see page 57*

Method
Follow Steps 1–5 of the General Method.

Recipes

Sanders Wood

(Pterocarpus santalinus)

A SMALL TREE FROM INDIA AND THE EAST INDIES, SANDERS WOOD IS PRIZED PRIMARILY FOR ITS RED HEARTWOOD, USED TO PRODUCE DYE.

General Method

1 Soak the wood chips overnight with enough water to cover.
2 Next day, add more water if necessary and slowly bring to the boil. Boil for 60 minutes.
3 Strain the liquid into the dyepot and add the yarn. If necessary, add more water to cover the yarn. Slowly bring up to the boil.
4 Boil for 45 minutes—the whole process should take about 2 hours.
5 When cool enough to handle, remove the yarn, wash in mild soapy water, and then rinse until the water runs clear.

Apricot

YARN: ALUM MORDANT

INGREDIENTS
- *Sanders wood chips: 100% of the yarn weight*
- *Yarn, alum-mordanted at 8%, see page 57*

Method
Follow Steps 1–5 of the General Method.

Dried Apricot

YARN: COPPER MORDANT

INGREDIENTS
- *Sanders wood chips: 100% of the yarn weight*
- *Yarn, copper-mordanted at 2%, see page 58*

Method
Follow Steps 1–5 of the General Method.

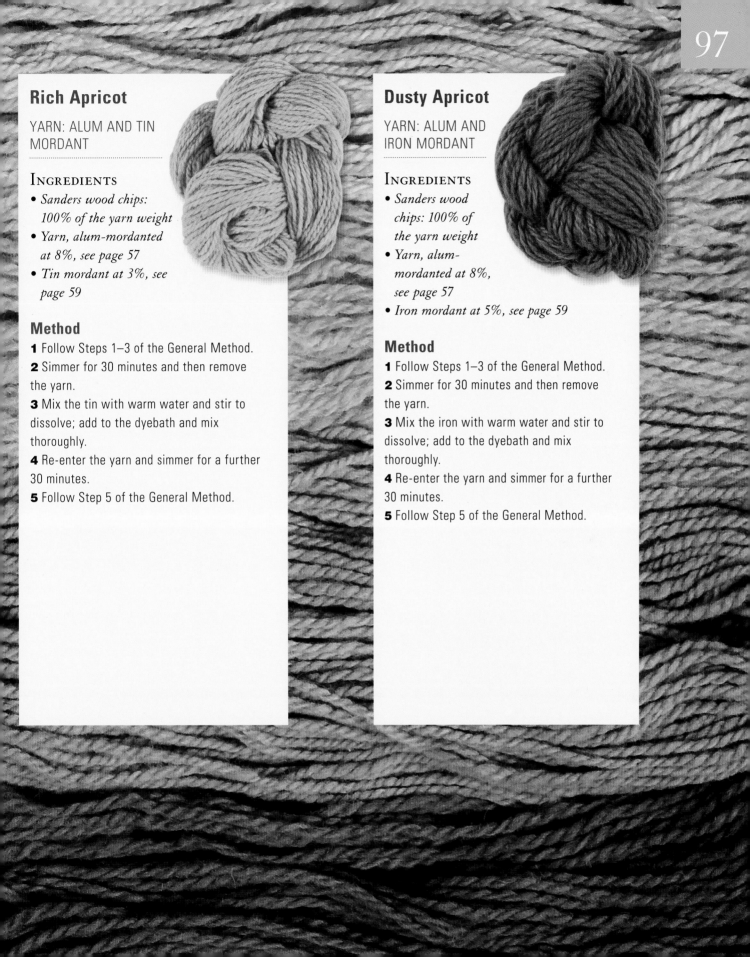

Rich Apricot

YARN: ALUM AND TIN MORDANT

INGREDIENTS

- *Sanders wood chips: 100% of the yarn weight*
- *Yarn, alum-mordanted at 8%, see page 57*
- *Tin mordant at 3%, see page 59*

Method

1 Follow Steps 1–3 of the General Method.
2 Simmer for 30 minutes and then remove the yarn.
3 Mix the tin with warm water and stir to dissolve; add to the dyebath and mix thoroughly.
4 Re-enter the yarn and simmer for a further 30 minutes.
5 Follow Step 5 of the General Method.

Dusty Apricot

YARN: ALUM AND IRON MORDANT

INGREDIENTS

- *Sanders wood chips: 100% of the yarn weight*
- *Yarn, alum-mordanted at 8%, see page 57*
- *Iron mordant at 5%, see page 59*

Method

1 Follow Steps 1–3 of the General Method.
2 Simmer for 30 minutes and then remove the yarn.
3 Mix the iron with warm water and stir to dissolve; add to the dyebath and mix thoroughly.
4 Re-enter the yarn and simmer for a further 30 minutes.
5 Follow Step 5 of the General Method.

chapter four

Recipes

Madder

(Rubia tinctorum)

MADDER TAKES THREE YEARS TO MATURE, SO IT IS IMPORTANT THAT THE ROOTS—PREFERABLY CHOPPED—ARE OF GOOD QUALITY. ALSO THE HARDER THE WATER USED, THE REDDER THE TONES.

General Method

1 Place your chopped roots in cold water in the dyepot and soak overnight. If using powder, paste with warm water and leave overnight.
2 Next day, add more water to the roots or the powder. Add the yarn and very slowly bring the water to a slow simmer at 140°F (60°C).
3 Simmer at that temperature for 1 to 2 hours.
4 Leave the yarn in the dyebath overnight.
5 Wash in mild soapy water and rinse until the water runs clear.

Brick Red

YARN: ALUM MORDANT

INGREDIENTS
• *Madder roots: 100% of the yarn weight*
• *Aged yarn, alum-mordanted at 8%, see page 57*

Method
Follow Steps 1–5 of the General Method.

Dark Khaki

YARN: ALUM AND IRON MORDANT

INGREDIENTS
- *Madder roots: 100% of the yarn weight*
- *Aged yarn, alum-mordanted at 8%, see page 57*
- *Iron mordant: At 5%, see page 59*

Method

1 Follow Steps 1–2 of the General Method.

2 Simmer at that temperature for 45 minutes. Remove the yarn.

3 Mix the iron with hot water and add to the dyebath, stirring well.

4 Replace yarn and simmer for 60 minutes.

5 Remove when cool enough to handle—do not leave overnight.

6 Follow Step 5 of the General Method.

Orange-red

YARN: ALUM AND TIN MORDANT

INGREDIENTS
- *Madder roots: 100% of the yarn weight*
- *Aged yarn, alum-mordanted at 8%, see page 57*
- *Tin mordant: At 3%, see page 59*

Method

1 Follow Steps 1–2 of the General Method.

2 Simmer at that temperature for 45 minutes. Remove the yarn.

3 Mix the tin with warm water and add to the dyebath, stirring well.

4 Replace the yarn and simmer for a further 60 minutes.

5 Remove when cool enough to handle—do not leave overnight.

6 Follow Step 5 of the General Method.

Rich Sand

YARN: COPPER MORDANT

INGREDIENTS
- *Madder roots: 100% of the yarn weight*
- *Yarn, copper-mordanted at 2%, see page 58*

Method

Follow Steps 1–5 of the General Method.

Recipes

Cochineal

(Dactylopius coccus)

IN THE EARLY SIXTEENTH CENTURY, SPANIARDS FOUND THE NATIVES OF MEXICO DRYING THE BODIES OF TINY INSECTS THAT LIVE ON THE NOPAL CACTUS AND GRINDING THEM INTO A POWDER READY FOR DYEING: THIS WAS KNOWN AS COCHINEAL.

General Method

1 Grind dried bodies to a powder if necessary.

2 Add ground cochineal to warm water and mix into a mush, making sure there are no lumps. Add to the dyepot. Place the yarn in the dyebath. If necessary, add more water to cover the yarn.

3 Heat gently, bringing the bath to a simmer over about 30 minutes.

4 Simmer for 60 minutes.

5 Leave yarn in the dyebath until cool enough to handle or overnight.

6 Rinse thoroughly to get rid of the cochineal powdery bits and then wash in mild soapy water. Rinse until the water runs clear.

NOTE: *The color depends on the quality of the cochineal and the quality of the water—the softer the better. If the color tends too much toward rose or pink, you must increase the amount of cochineal or lengthen the dyeing time.*

Blue-red

YARN: ALUM
MORDANT

INGREDIENTS

- *Ground cochineal: 30% of the yarn weight*
- *Yarn, alum-mordanted at 8%, see page 57*

Method

Follow Steps 1–6 of the General Method.

Maroon-red

YARN: COPPER
MORDANT

INGREDIENTS

- *Ground cochineal: 30% of the yarn weight*
- *Yarn, copper-mordanted at 2%, see page 58*

Method

Follow Steps 1–6 of the General Method.

Rich red

YARN: ALUM AND TIN
MORDANT

INGREDIENTS

- *Ground cochineal: 30% of the yarn weight*
- *Yarn, alum-mordanted at 8%, see page 57*
- *Tin mordant: At 3%, see page 59*

Method

1 Follow Steps 1–3 of the General Method.
2 Simmer for 30 minutes and remove the yarn.
3 Mix tin with warm water, add to the dyebath, and stir thoroughly.
4 Place the yarn back in the dyebath and simmer for a further 30 minutes or more.
5 Follow Steps 5–6 of the General Method.

Purple-red

YARN: ALUM AND IRON
MORDANT

INGREDIENTS

- *Ground cochineal: 30% of the yarn weight*
- *Yarn, alum-mordanted at 8%, see page 57*
- *Iron mordant: At 5%, see page 59*

Method

1 Follow Steps 1–3 of the General Method.
2 When the yarn has simmered for 30 minutes, take it out, mix iron with warm water, add to the dyebath, and stir thoroughly.
3 Place the yarn back in the dyebath. Simmer for a further 30 minutes.
4 Follow Steps 5–6 of the General Method.

chapter four

Recipes

Alkanet

(Alkanna tinctoria)

ALKANET LOST ITS POPULARITY ONCE MADDER WAS INTRODUCED. HOWEVER, THESE RECIPES GIVE A REASONABLE LIGHT- AND WASH-FASTNESS. THE CHOPPED ROOTS CAN BE BOUGHT FROM MOST DYESTUFF SELLERS.

General Method

1 Soak the alkanet roots overnight, or for at least 12 hours. Place the roots in a saucepan with the soaking water. Add more water to cover if necessary. Boil for at least 45 to 60 minutes.

2 Cool, then strain liquid into the dyepot.

3 Add acetic acid or vinegar and mix well.

4 Place yarn in dyebath. If necessary, add more water to cover the yarn.

5 Heat gently, bringing the bath to just under boiling point over a period of 60 minutes. Simmer for 45 minutes.

6 When the yarn is cool enough to handle, wash in mild soapy water. Rinse well until color stops running.

NOTE: *Save your dyebaths (called exhaust baths) from the first recipe of each dye plant.*

Purple-brown

YARN: NO MORDANT

INGREDIENTS

- *Alkanet root: 100% of the yarn weight, soaked overnight or for at least 12 hours*
- *Washed yarn*
- *Acetic acid: At 5% or*
- *Vinegar: At 8%*

Method

Follow Steps 1–6 of the General Method.

Purple-gray

YARN: ALUM AND IRON MORDANT

INGREDIENTS

- *Alkanet root: 100% of the yarn weight, soaked overnight or for at least 12 hours*
- *Yarn, alum-mordanted at 8%, see page 57*
- *Iron mordant at 5%, see page 59*
- *Acetic acid: At 5% (or vinegar: At 8%)*

Method

1 Follow Steps 1–4 of the General Method.

2 Heat gently, bringing the bath to just under boiling point over 60 minutes. Take out the yarn 30 minutes before the dyeing is complete.

3 Mix iron in warm water and add to the dyebath. Stir thoroughly.

4 Put the yarn back in the bath and simmer for 30 minutes.

5 Follow Step 6 of the General Method.

Red-tinged Khaki

YARN: COPPER MORDANT

INGREDIENTS

- *100% of the yarn weight, soaked overnight or for at least 12 hours*
- *Yarn, copper-mordanted at 2%*
- *Acetic acid: At 5% or*
- *Vinegar: At 8%*

Method

1 Follow Steps 1–4 of the General Method.
2 Heat gently, bringing the bath to just under boiling point over 60 minutes. Take out the yarn 30 minutes before the dyeing is complete.
3 Mix iron in warm water and add to the dyebath. Stir thoroughly.
4 Put the yarn back in the bath and simmer for 30 minutes.
5 Follow Step 6 of the General Method.

Khaki

YARN: COPPER AND IRON MORDANT

INGREDIENTS

- *Alkanet root: 100% of the yarn weight, soaked overnight or for at least 12 hours*
- *Yarn, copper-mordanted at 2%*
- *Acetic acid: At 5% or*
- *Vinegar: At 8%*
- *Iron mordant: At 5%*

Method

1 Follow Steps 1–4 of the General Method.
2 Simmer for 30 minutes and take out the yarn.
3 Mix iron with warm water and stir into the dyebath, mixing thoroughly.
4 Re-enter the yarn and simmer for a further 30 minutes.
5 Follow Step 6 of the General Method.

chapter four

Recipes

Logwood

(Haematoxylum campechianum)

LOGWOOD IS LIGHT-SENSITIVE, SO IT NEEDS
CAREFUL MORDANTING; IT IS ALSO
SENSITIVE TO WATER QUALITY. ACIDIC
WATER WILL GIVE REDDER TONES WHILE
ALKALINE WATER WILL GIVE BLUER ONES.

General Method

1 Soak chips overnight in cold water. Next day add water to cover the chips and bring to a vigorous boil. Boil for 30 minutes.

2 When cool, strain liquor into dyepot. Add yarn and more water if necessary to completely submerge the yarn.

3 Slowly bring the dyebath to just under the boiling point.

4 Simmer for at least 30 minutes or until the desired color is reached, but no longer than 60 minutes.

5 When cool enough to handle, wash the yarn in mild soapy water and then rinse until the water runs clear.

Royal Purple

YARN: ALUM MORDANT

Ingredients
- *Logwood chips: 50% of the yarn weight*
- *Yarn, alum-mordanted at 24%, see page 57*

Method
Follow Steps 1–5 of the General Method.

Blue-purple

YARN: COPPER MORDANT

Ingredients
- *Logwood chips: 50% of the yarn weight*
- *Yarn, copper-mordanted at 2%, see page 58*

Method
Follow Steps 1–5 of the General Method.

Bright Purple

YARN: ALUM AND TIN MORDANT

Ingredients
- *Logwood chips: 50% of the yarn weight*
- *Yarn, alum-mordanted at 24%, see page 57*
- *Tin mordant: At 3%, see page 59*

Method
1 Follow Steps 1–3 of the General Method.
2 Simmer for 30 minutes. Remove the yarn.
3 Mix the tin with warm water and add to the dyebath, mixing well.
4 Replace the yarn and simmer for 30 minutes.
5 Follow Step 5 of the General Method.

Almost Black

YARN: ALUM AND IRON MORDANT

Ingredients
- *Logwood chips: 50% of the yarn weight*
- *Yarn, alum-mordanted at 24%, see page 57*
- *Iron mordant: At 5%, see page 59*

Method
1 Follow Steps 1–3 of the General Method.
2 Simmer for 30 minutes. Remove the yarn.
3 Dissolve iron with hot water, add to the dyebath and mix well.
4 Replace the yarn and simmer for a further 30 minutes.
5 Follow Step 5 of the General Method.

Recipes

Fustic

(Chlorophora tinctoria)

FUSTIC (SOMETIMES KNOWN AS OLD FUSTIC) IS HIGH IN TANNIC ACID, WHICH MAKES IT GOOD FOR COTTON DYEING AS WELL AS FOR WOOL AND SILK.

General Method

1 Put the fustic chips in a leg from an old pair of panty hose. Place in a dyepot of cold water—enough to cover the chips completely.

2 Bring gently to the boil and simmer for 45 to 60 minutes.

3 Cool in the pot and then remove the fustic chips. Add enough warm water to cover the fabric to be dyed.

4 Wet the fabric and add it to the dyebath. Slowly bring to the boil over 30 to 45 minutes. Simmer for 45 to 60 minutes.

5 Stir the fabric frequently so all the surfaces pick up the dye color evenly, but make sure that the fabric remains underneath the water surface at all times.

6 During the dyeing you can check the color of the fabric by rinsing under running cold tap water and then squeezing tightly dry.

7 When you have the color you require, rinse well in warm water and then wash in warm water using a pH-neutral soap. Rinse well again in warm water and air-dry.

Yellow

WOOL: ALUM AND
TIN MORDANT

INGREDIENTS
- *Fustic chips:
  50–100% to dry
  weight of fabric*
- *Wool, alum-
  mordanted at 8%, see page 57*
- *Tin mordant: At 7%, see page 59*

Method
Follow Steps 1–7 of the General Method.

VARIATION: *Fustic can also be used with copper or chrome mordants to change the color.*

Sandy Yellow

WOOL: ALUM AND
IRON MORDANT

INGREDIENTS
- *Fustic chips:
  20–50% to dry
  weight of fabric*
- *Wool, alum-
  mordanted at 8%, see page 57*
- *Iron mordant: At 5%, see page 59*

Method
Follow Steps 1–7 of the General Method.

VARIATION: *Dye cotton fabric with this dye as well. It is high in tannic acid, which will help with the color intensity and lightfastness of cotton.*

Pale Yellow

SILK: ALUM
MORDANT

INGREDIENTS
- *Fustic chips:
  20–50% to dry
  weight of fabric*
- *Silk, alum-
  mordanted at 8%, see page 57*

Method
Follow Steps 1–7 of the General Method.

VARIATION: *Matte, shiny, transparent, and opaque silk fabrics will all produce different shades when dyed.*

Light Yellow

WOOL: ALUM
MORDANT

INGREDIENTS
- *Fustic chips:
  20–50% to dry
  weight of fabric*
- *Wool, alum-
  mordanted at 8%, see page 57*

Method
Follow Steps 1–7 of the General Method.

VARIATION: *Soak the fustic chips overnight and then boil and simmer to release the color.*

chapter four

Recipes

Weld

(Reseda luteola)

ONE OF THE OLDEST AND FASTEST OF THE YELLOW DYES, WELD TURNS WOOL AND SILK AN EXTREMELY BRIGHT YELLOW; IT HAS ALSO BEEN USED TO DYE LEATHER AND HORN.

General Method

1 Place the weld in a saucepan, add enough hot water to dissolve, and heat to a maximum of 160°F (70°C).
2 Simmer at this temperature for 30 to 120 minutes. Cool in the saucepan.
3 Strain the dye water into a dyepot. Add enough warm water to allow free movement of the fabric below the water.
4 Wet the fabric and add it to the dyebath. Slowly raise the temperature to a maximum of 160°F (70°C) over 20 to 30 minutes. Simmer at this temperature for 45 to 60 minutes.
5 Stir the fabric frequently so all the surfaces pick up the dye color evenly, but make sure that the fabric remains underneath the water surface at all times.
6 During the dyeing you can check the color of the fabric by rinsing under running cold tap water and then squeezing tightly dry.
7 When you have the color you require, rinse well in warm water and then wash in warm water using a pH-neutral soap. Rinse well again in warm water and air-dry.

Chalk

WOOL: NO MORDANT

INGREDIENTS
- *Dried weld: 10–20% to dry weight of fabric*
- *Wool*
- *Acetic acid at 5% or*
- *Vinegar: At 8%*
- *Indigo vat, see pages 60–64*

Method

1 Follow Steps 1–3 of the General Method.
2 Wet the fabric and add it to the dyepot. Slowly raise the temperature to just below boiling point over 20 to 30 minutes. Simmer for 45 to 60 minutes.
3 Follow Steps 5–6 of the General Method.
4 Dip and oxidize in the indigo vat for 3 to 10 minutes. Remove from the vat and oxidize for 3 to 10 minutes to overdye to green.
5 Rinse well in warm water.
6 Soak in a bath of diluted acetic acid or white vinegar for 10 minutes to neutralize the caustic soda in the indigo vat.
7 Rinse well in warm water and then wash in warm water using a pH-neutral soap. Rinse well again in warm water and air-dry

VARIATION: *Vary the length of the overdyeing times to achieve different shades of green.*

SEE ALSO:
LEAVES, PAGE 48

Orange-yellow

WOOL: ALUM
MORDANT

INGREDIENTS
- *Fresh weld: 100–200% to dry weight of fabric*
- *Wool, alum-mordanted at 8%, see page 57*

Method
1 Place the weld in a saucepan, cover with warm water, and leave to soak overnight. Gently heat to just below boiling point.
2 Follow Steps 2–3 of the General Method.
3 Wet the fabric and add it to the dyebath. Slowly raise the temperature to just below boiling point over 20 to 30 minutes. Simmer for 45 to 120 minutes, depending on the depth of shade required.
4 Follow Steps 5–7 of the General Method.

VARIATION: *Different parts of the plant have different amounts of color within them. Try using just the fresh seeds or just the fresh leaves and thin stalks. Different strains of weld will also produce different tones, as will picking the plant at different times—mid- or late summer, after the rain or not, will all affect the tone and color released from the plant.*

Bright Yellow

SILK: ALUM
MORDANT

INGREDIENTS
- *Dried weld: 30–100% to dry weight of fabric*
- *Silk, alum-mordanted at 8%, see page 57*

Method
1 Follow Steps 1–3 of the General Method.
2 Wet the fabric and add it to the dyebath. Slowly raise the temperature to just below boiling point over 20 to 30 minutes. Simmer for 45 to 60 minutes.
3 Follow Steps 5–7 of the General Method.

VARIATION: *Adding calcium carbonate to the dyepot will give brighter lemon shades.*

Medium Yellow

WOOL: ALUM
MORDANT

INGREDIENTS
- *Dried weld: 30–100% to dry weight of fabric*
- *Wool, alum-mordanted at 8%, see page 57*

Method
Follow Steps 1–7 of the General Method.

VARIATION: *Leave the fabrics in the dyebath for only 10–15 minutes for really pale shades or use a smaller percentage of dried weld to fabric weight.*

chapter four

Recipes

Henna

(Lawsonia inermis)

HENNA HAS BEEN USED FOR CENTURIES AS A DYE FOR THE HAIR, BODY, AND FABRICS. MOST PHARMACIES WITH A HAIR-DYEING SECTION STOCK HENNA IN POWDER FORM.

General Method

1 Paste the henna powder with a little hot water. Add to a dyepot of warm water—enough to easily cover the fabric. Stir thoroughly until fully dissolved.

2 Wet the fabric and add it to the dyebath. Slowly bring to the boil over 20 to 30 minutes. Simmer for 45 to 60 minutes.

3 Stir the fabric frequently so all the surfaces pick up the dye color evenly, but make sure that the fabric remains fully submerged at all times.

4 During the dyeing you can check the color of the fabric by rinsing it under running cold tap water and then squeezing tightly dry.

5 When you have the color you require, rinse well in warm water and then wash in warm water using a pH-neutral soap. Rinse well again in warm water and air-dry. If you want a paler shade, use even less henna—try 20% or 30%.

Beige

WOOL: NO MORDANT

INGREDIENTS
- *Henna: 50% to dry weight of fabric*
- *Wool*

Method
Follow Steps 1–5 of the General Method.

VARIATION: *Different tones of color can be achieved by using different brands of henna and even henna from different countries.*

Beige-brown

WOOL: ALUM MORDANT

INGREDIENTS
- *Henna: 50% to dry weight of fabric*
- *Wool, alum-mordanted at 25%, see page 57*

Method
Follow Steps 1–5 of the General Method.

VARIATION: *Leave the fabric in the henna dyepot for several hours to achieve an even deeper color.*

Recipes

Heather

(Calluna vulgaris)

HEATHER HAS BEEN USED FOR CENTURIES AS A DYESTUFF, MAINLY BECAUSE PEOPLE COULD PICK IT FREELY. IT GIVES A BEIGE TO TAN COLOR, WHICH OFTEN FADES IN BRIGHT LIGHT.

General Method

1 Put the heather in the leg of an old pair of panty hose. Place in a dyepot of cold water—enough to cover the heather completely.

2 Bring gently to the boil. Simmer for 45 to 60 minutes.

3 Cool in the pot and then remove the heather. Add enough warm water to cover the fabric to be dyed.

4 Wet the fabric and add it to the dyebath. Slowly bring to the boil over 30 to 45 minutes. Simmer for 45 to 60 minutes.

5 Stir the fabric frequently so all the surfaces pick up the dye color evenly, but make sure that the fabric remains underneath the water surface at all times.

6 During the dyeing you can check the color of the fabric by rinsing under running cold tap water and then squeezing tightly dry.

7 When you have the color you require, rinse well in warm water and then wash in warm water using a pH-neutral soap. Rinse well again in warm water and air-dry.

Beige-white

WOOL: ALUM MORDANT

INGREDIENTS
- *Dried heather: 50–100% to dry weight of fabric*
- *Wool, alum-mordanted at 8%, see page 57*

Method
Follow Steps 1–7 of the General Method.

VARIATION: *Using different weights of wool fabric will result in different depths of color.*

Beige-yellow

WOOL: ALUM MORDANT

INGREDIENTS
- *Fresh heather: 100–200% to dry weight of fabric*
- *Wool, alum-mordanted at 8%, see page 57*

Method
Follow Steps 1–7 of the General Method.

VARIATION: *If you can get only a small amount of fresh heather, try adding some of the stems as well as the flowers, bearing in mind that the stems will affect the final color.*

Recipes

Cutch

(Acacia catechu)

CUTCH WILL DYE WOOL, SILK, COTTON, AND EVEN LEATHER A VARIETY OF SHADES OF ORANGE THROUGH TO BROWN AND, WITH DIFFERENT MORDANTS AND OTHER DYES, GRAYS THROUGH TO ALMOST BLACK.

General Method

1 Paste the cutch powder with a little hot water and add to a dyepot of warm water—enough to easily cover the fabric. Stir thoroughly until fully dissolved.

2 Bring to the boil and simmer for 30 minutes. Cool in the dyepot.

3 Wet the fabric and add it to the dyebath. Slowly bring to the boil over 20 to 30 minutes. Simmer for 45 to 60 minutes.

4 Stir the fabric frequently so all the surfaces pick up the dye color evenly, but make sure that the fabric remains underneath the water surface at all times.

5 During the dyeing you can check the color of the fabric by rinsing under running cold tap water and then squeezing tightly dry.

6 When you have the color you require, rinse well in warm water and then wash in warm water using a pH-neutral soap. Rinse well again in warm water and air-dry.

Orange-red

WOOL: ALUM MORDANT

INGREDIENTS

- *Cutch powder: 100% to dry weight of fabric*
- *Wool, alum-mordanted at 8%, see page 57*

Method

Follow Steps 1–6 of the General Method.

VARIATION: *Try using the powder at different percentages—say 20% to 60%—to produce other shades of this color.*

Orange-brown

WOOL: ALUM AND IRON MORDANT

INGREDIENTS
- *Cutch powder: 100% to dry weight of fabric*
- *Wool, alum-mordanted at 8%, see page 57*
- *Iron mordant: At 5%, see page 59*

Method
1 Follow Steps 1–3 of the General Method.
2 About 20 to 30 minutes before the end of dyeing, remove the fabric and add the iron mordant to the dyebath, stirring well.
3 Replace the fabric and continue dyeing until the correct color is achieved.
4 Follow Steps 4–6 of the General Method.

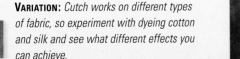
VARIATION: *Cutch works on different types of fabric, so experiment with dyeing cotton and silk and see what different effects you can achieve.*

Tangerine Orange

WOOL: ALUM MORDANT

INGREDIENTS
- *Cutch powder: 100% to dry weight of fabric*
- *Wool, pre-dyed with weld (see page 108), alum-mordanted at 8% (see page 57)*

Method
Follow Steps 1–6 of the General Method.

VARIATION: *Instead of weld, add cutch to cochineal, madder, or indigo. All will give differing colors and depths of color depending on the percentages of dye used.*

Orange-yellow

WOOL: NO MORDANT

INGREDIENTS
- *Cutch powder: 100% to dry weight of fabric*
- *Wool*

Method
Follow Steps 1–6 of the General Method.

VARIATION: *To intensify the color, leave the cutch powder to soak overnight before adding the fabric.*

Recipes

Madder

(Rubia tinctorum)

RED MADDER IS STILL USED IN THE PRODUCTION OF CARPETS. IT WORKS ON ANIMAL AND VEGETABLE FIBERS AND CAN ALSO BE MADE INTO A PRINTING PASTE FOR PATTERNING FABRICS.

General Method

1 Place your chopped roots in cold water in the dyepot and soak overnight. If using powder, paste with warm water and leave overnight. Next day, add more water to the roots or the powder.

2 Wet the fabric and place in the dyebath. Slowly raise the temperature to no more than 140°F (60°C) over 20 to 30 minutes. Simmer at this temperature for 60 to 90 minutes.

3 Stir the fabric frequently so all the surfaces pick up the dye color evenly, but make sure that the fabric remains underneath the water surface at all times.

4 During the dyeing you can check the color of the fabric by rinsing under running cold tap water and then squeezing tightly dry.

5 Place back in the dyebath if you require a stronger color.

6 When you have the color you want, rinse well in warm water and then wash in warm water using a pH-neutral soap. Rinse well again in warm water and air-dry.

▶ SEE ALSO:
ROOTS, PAGE 52

Red-brown

WOOL: ALUM AND
IRON MORDANT

INGREDIENTS

- *Madder powder:
  100% to dry weight
  of fabric*
- *Wool, alum-
  mordanted at 8%, see page 57*
- *Iron mordant: At 5%, see page 59*

Method

Follow Steps 1–6 of the General Method.

VARIATION: *Instead of the iron mordant you can dip and oxidize the madder-dyed fabric in an indigo vat for 2 to 5 minutes to brown the fabric.*

Muted Pink

WOOL: NO MORDANT

INGREDIENTS

- *Madder powder:
  100% to dry weight
  of fabric*
- *Wool*

Method

Follow Steps 1–6 of the General Method.

VARIATION: *By varying the length of time in the dyebath, the strength of the dyebath, or the type of fabric you use, you can achieve different shades of pink.*

Orange-cream

WOOL: ALUM
MORDANT

INGREDIENTS

- *Madder powder:
  100% to dry weight
  of fabric*
- *Wool, alum-
  mordanted at 8%, see page 57*

Method

Follow Steps 1–6 of the General Method.

VARIATION: *If the fabric is left overnight to cool and absorb more color, the result can be a patchy pick-up of dye. But it is worth experimenting with different fabric types, as some will pick up the dye evenly when not stirred frequently.*

Bright Red

WOOL: ALUM AND
TIN MORDANT

INGREDIENTS

- *Madder powder:
  100% to dry weight
  of fabric*
- *Wool, alum-
  mordanted at 8%, see page 57*
- *Tin mordant: At 7%, see page 59*

Method

Follow Steps 1–6 of the General Method.

VARIATION: *To increase the intensity of the red, you can also overdye with cochineal.*

Recipes

Safflower

(Carthamus tinctorius)

SAFFLOWER DYE WILL TURN SILK
YELLOW AND COTTON RED. THE DYE WAS
ORIGINALLY USED TO DYE THE COTTON
TAPE USED FOR LEGAL DOCUMENTS, HENCE
THE EXPRESSION "RED TAPE."

General Method

1 Place the safflower petals in a saucepan, cover with hot water, and bring to the boil.
2 Simmer for 30 minutes. Cool in the saucepan.
3 Strain the dye water through panty hose. Place the panty hose with the safflower petals in a dyepot. Add enough warm water to allow free movement of the fabric below the water.
4 Wet the fabric and add it to the dyebath. Slowly bring to the boil over 20 to 30 minutes. Simmer for 60 to 90 minutes.
5 Stir the fabric frequently so all the surfaces pick up the dye color evenly, but make sure that the fabric remains underneath the water surface at all times.
6 During the dyeing you can check the color of the fabric by rinsing under running cold tap water and then squeezing tightly dry.
7 When you have the color you require, rinse well in warm water and then wash in warm water using a pH-neutral soap. Rinse well again in warm water and air-dry.

Palest Cream

SILK: NO MORDANT

INGREDIENTS
• *Safflower petals: 100–200% to dry weight of fabric*
• *Silk*

Method
Follow Steps 1–7 of the General Method.

VARIATION: *For a paler color, remove the fabric after 15–20 minutes of simmering.*

Muted Yellow

COTTON: ALUM MORDANT

INGREDIENTS
• *Safflower petals: 100–200% to dry weight of fabric*
• *Cottom, alum-mordanted at 8%, see page 57*

Method
Follow Steps 1–7 of the General Method.

VARIATION: *A different weight of cotton will give a very different tone when dyed in this dyepot.*

Hint of Pink

SILK: NO MORDANT

Ingredients
- *Safflower petals: 100–200% to dry weight of fabric*
- *Silk*
- *Washing soda*
- *Vinegar*

Method

1 Follow Steps 1–7 of the General Method.

2 Make a new dyebath with the used safflower petals in the panty hose. Add enough cold water to allow free movement of the fabric below the water. Add enough washing soda (alkali) to change the pH level of the dyebath to 11. Leave to settle for 60 minutes.

3 Neutralize the dyebath with a vinegar solution (acid) to change the pH level to 6. Add the cotton fabric.

4 Leave the fabric to dye cold in this bath for 2 to 4 hours or overnight if possible.

5 Follow steps 5–7 of the General Method.

VARIATION: *For a paler color remove the fabric early from the dyebath or add less dye to the initial bath.*

Soft Pink

COTTON: NO MORDANT

Ingredients
- *Dried safflower: 50–100% to dry weight of fabric*
- *Cotton*
- *Washing soda*
- *Vinegar*

Method

1 Follow Steps 1–7 of the General Method.

2 Make a new dyebath with the used safflower petals in the panty hose. Add enough cold water to allow free movement of the fabric below the water. Add enough washing soda (alkali) to change the pH level of the dyepot to 11. Leave to settle for 60 minutes.

3 Neutralize the dyepot with a vinegar solution (acid) to change the pH level to 6. Add the cotton fabric.

4 Leave the fabric to dye cold in this bath for 2 to 4 hours or overnight if possible.

5 Follow steps 5–7 of the General Method.

VARIATION: *The fabric was left in this dyebath overnight—notice how it gives a more intense color.*

Recipes

Cochineal

(Dactylopius coccus)

COCHINEAL DYE COMES FROM THE DRIED BODIES OF INSECTS THAT LIVE ON CERTAIN PRICKLY PEAR CACTI NATIVE TO THE TROPICAL REGIONS OF SOUTH AND CENTRAL AMERICA.

General Method

1 Grind the cochineal to powder in a coffee grinder.

2 Paste this powder with a little hot water and add to a dyepot of warm water—enough to easily cover the fabric. Stir thoroughly until fully dissolved.

3 Wet the fabric and add it to the dyebath. Slowly bring to the boil over 20 to 30 minutes. Simmer for 45 to 60 minutes.

4 Stir the fabric frequently so all the surfaces pick up the dye color evenly, but make sure that the fabric remains underneath the water surface at all times.

5 During the dyeing you can check the color of the fabric by rinsing under running cold tap water and then squeezing tightly dry.

6 When you have the color you require, rinse well in warm water and then wash in warm water using a pH-neutral soap. Rinse well again in warm water and air-dry.

Purple-red

WOOL: ALUM MORDANT

INGREDIENTS

- *Dried cochineal: 10–20% to dry weight of fabric*
- *Wool, alum-mordanted at 8%, see page 57*
- *Indigo vat, see pages 60–64*

Method

1 Follow Steps 1–5 of the General Method.

2 Overdye by dipping and oxidizing from an indigo vat for 3 to 10 minutes to achieve varying shades of purple.

3 Follow Step 6 of the General Method.

VARIATION: *For deeper shades, dip and oxidize for longer periods of time in the indigo vat.*

Cream-pink

WOOL: NO MORDANT

INGREDIENTS
- *Dried cochineal: 5–10% to dry weight of fabric*
- *Wool*

Method
Follow Steps 1–6 of the General Method.

VARIATION: *Try using cochineal from a previous dyepot. It is a hard dye to exhaust and a previously well-used bath often produces pale colors.*

Watermelon Red

WOOL: ALUM AND TIN MORDANT

INGREDIENTS
- *Dried cochineal: 10–20% to dry weight of fabric*
- *Wool, alum-mordanted at 8%, see page 57*
- *Oxalic acid: At 8%*
- *Tin mordant: At 7%, see page 59*

Method
1 Follow Steps 1–2 of the General Method.
2 Dissolve the oxalic acid and the tin mordant in the dyebath and stir thoroughly.
3 Follow Steps 3–6 of the General Method.

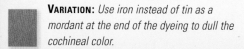

VARIATION: *Use iron instead of tin as a mordant at the end of the dyeing to dull the cochineal color.*

Baby Pink

WOOL: ALUM MORDANT

INGREDIENTS
- *Dried cochineal: 5–10% to dry weight of fabric*
- *Wool, alum-mordanted at 8%, see page 57*

Method
Follow Steps 1–6 of the General Method.

VARIATION: *Try adding some tartaric acid to the dyepot to release more color from the dye.*

Recipes

Alkanet

(Alkanna tinctoria)

ALKANET GIVES COLORS RANGING FROM GRAY THROUGH TO MAUVE AND PURPLE, AND IT IS OFTEN USED WITH OTHER NATURAL DYES TO INCREASE THE COLOR RANGE.

General Method

1 Grind the root to powder in a coffee grinder.

2 Paste this powder with a little hot water and add to a dyepot of warm water—enough to easily cover the fabric. Stir thoroughly until fully dissolved.

3 Wet the fabric and add it to the dyebath. Slowly bring to the boil over 20 to 30 minutes. Simmer for 45 to 60 minutes.

4 Stir the fabric frequently so that all the surfaces pick up the dye color evenly, but make sure that the fabric remains underneath the water surface at all times.

5 During the dyeing you can check the color of the fabric by rinsing under running cold tap water and then squeezing tightly dry.

6 When you have the color you require, rinse well in warm water and then wash in warm water using a pH-neutral soap. Rinse well again in warm water and air-dry.

Pale Gray

WOOL: ALUM MORDANT

INGREDIENTS

- *Alkanet root: 50–100% to dry weight of fabric*
- *Wool, alum-mordanted at 8%, see page 57*

Method

Follow Steps 1–6 of the General Method.

VARIATION: *For a darker gray, leave the fabric in the dyebath for a longer period of time.*

Purple-red

WOOL: ALUM AND
IRON MORDANT

Ingredients
- *Alkanet root:*
  50–100%
  to dry weight
  of fabric
- *Wool, alum-mordanted at 8%, see*
  page 57
- *Iron mordant: At 5%, see page 59*

Method
Follow Steps 1–6 of the General Method.

Variation: *You can vary the color depending on whether you choose 50% or 100% of dye powder.*

Medium-gray

WOOL: ALUM AND
TIN MORDANT

Ingredients
- *Alkanet root:*
  50–100% to dry
  weight of fabric
- *Wool, alum-*
  mordanted at 8%, see
  page 57
- *Tin mordant: At 5%, see page 59*

Method
1 Follow Steps 1–3 of the General Method.
2 About 20 to 30 minutes before the end of dyeing, remove the fabric and add the tin mordant to the dyebath, stirring well.
3 Follow Steps 4–6 of the General Method.

Variation: *Leaving the fabric in the tin after adding the mordant will change the tone achieved.*

Dark Purple

WOOL: ALUM MORDANT AND INDIGO

Ingredients
- *Alkanet root: 50–100% to dry*
  weight of fabric
- *Wool, alum-mordanted at 8%, see*
  page 57
- *Indigo dye vat, see pages 60–64*

Method
1 Follow Steps 1–5 of the General Method.
2 Dip and oxidize the fabric for 5 to 10 minutes in the indigo vat following the instructions on pages 60–64.
3 Follow Step 6 of the General Method.

Variation: *Vary the length of time in the indigo bath to achieve a deeper color.*

Recipes

Logwood

(Haematoxylum campechianum)

LOGWOOD IS AVAILABLE AS CHIPS OR SHAVINGS, WHICH GIVE A STRONGER MORE INTENSE BLACK COLOR ON COTTON. IT IS A NATIVE OF MEXICO AND CENTRAL AMERICA.

General Method

1 Put the logwood in the leg of an old pair of panty hose. Place in a saucepan of cold water—enough to easily cover the logwood. Soak overnight.

2 Bring to the boil slowly over 20 to 30 minutes. Simmer for 30 minutes. Cool in the saucepan.

3 Strain the dye water into a dyepot and add enough warm water to allow free movement of the fabric below the water.

4 Wet the fabric and add it to the dyebath. Slowly bring to the boil over 20 to 30 minutes. Simmer for 45 to 60 minutes.

5 Stir the fabric frequently so all the surfaces pick up the dye color evenly, but make sure that the fabric remains underneath the water surface at all times.

6 During the dyeing you can check the color of the fabric by rinsing under running cold tap water and then squeezing tightly dry.

7 When you have the color you require, rinse well in warm water and then wash in warm water using a pH-neutral soap. Rinse well again in warm water and air-dry.

Dark Gray

WOOL: ALUM AND IRON MORDANT

INGREDIENTS

- *Logwood: 50–100% to dry weight of fabric*
- *Wool, alum-mordanted at 8%, see page 57*
- *Iron mordant: At 5%, see page 59*

Method

1 Follow Steps 1–4 of the General Method.

2 20 to 30 minutes before the end of dyeing, remove the fabric. Add the iron mordant to the dyebath, stirring well.

3 Follow Steps 5–7 of the General Method.

VARIATION: *If you use copper as a final mordant, you can alter the tone of gray you achieve.*

Lavender

WOOL: ALUM
MORDANT

Ingredients
- *Logwood: 20–50%*
  to dry weight
  of fabric
- *Wool, alum-*
  mordanted at 8%, see
  page 57

Method
Follow Steps 1–7 of the General Method.

Variation: *Removing the fabric from the dyebath early will result in a more subtle lavender.*

Almost Black

COTTON: ALUM AND
IRON MORDANT

Ingredients
- *Logwood: 50–100%*
  to dry weight
  of fabric
- *Cotton, alum-mordanted at 25%,*
  see page 57
- *Fustic dyepot, see page 106*
- *Iron mordant: At 5%, see page 59*

Method
1 Follow Steps 1–4 of the General Method.
2 Overdye in a fustic dyebath to turn the dark blue to almost black. About 20 to 30 minutes before the end of dyeing, remove the fabric and add the iron mordant to the dyebath, stirring well.
3 Follow Steps 5–7 of the General Method.

Variation: *Over-dyeing in indigo can help to achieve a denser black.*

Purple

COTTON: ALUM
MORDANT

Ingredients
- *Logwood: 50–100%*
  to dry weight
  of fabric
- *Cotton, alum-*
  mordanted at 8%, see page 57

Method
Follow Steps 1–7 of the General Method.

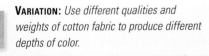

Variation: *Use different qualities and weights of cotton fabric to produce different depths of color.*

Recipes

Indigo

INDIGO IS ONE OF THE OLDEST TEXTILE DYES AND IS STILL IN COMMON USE. BLUE DENIM JEANS, THE ICONIC CLOTHING ITEM INVENTED BY LEVI STRAUSS IN THE LATE NINETEENTH CENTURY, OWE A LARGE PART OF THEIR IDENTITY AND SUCCESS TO INDIGO.

General Method (for Wools and Silks)

1 Prepare the indigo vat following the instructions on pages 60–64. If there is a skin or bloom on the vat carefully remove it with a kitchen towel.

2 Gently immerse wet fabric for 1 minute in the vat so as not to add any oxygen to the vat.

3 The fabric should hang freely so all surfaces are exposed to the indigo liquid.

4 Gently move and turn the immersed fabric underneath the surface to aid even dyeing.

5 Gently remove the fabric from the vat. Oxidize in the air for 1 minute. Make sure that the fabric remains open and flat while it is out of the vat.

6 Dip the fabric back in the vat for 1 minute.

7 Remove from the vat and oxidize for 1 minute.

8 Repeat Steps 6 and 7 until 10 dips and oxidizations have been completed.

9 Rinse well in warm water.

10 Soak in a bath of diluted acetic acid or white vinegar for 10 minutes to neutralize the caustic soda in the vat.

11 Rinse well in warm water and then wash in warm water using a pH-neutral soap. Rinse well again in warm water and air-dry.

Forest Green

WOOL: ALUM MORDANT

INGREDIENTS

- *Indigo vat, see pages 60–64*
- *Wool, alum-mordanted at 8% (see page 57), pre-dyed with weld (see page 108)*
- *Neutralizing bath: ¼ tsp (1 ml) acetic acid at 20%, or a small amount of white vinegar in 2 pt (1 l) of cold water*

Method

1 Follow Steps 1–7 of the General Method.

2 Repeat Steps 6 and 7 until three dips and oxidizations have been completed.

3 Follow Steps 9–11 of the General Method.

VARIATION: *Many natural-dyed fabrics can be overdyed with indigo to make colors such as green and also to deepen colors—browns and reds will take on a much darker tone. It is worth testing natural-dyed fabrics to see what changes can be made. Record the dip and oxidization time for each color so you can repeat if required.*

⊙ SEE ALSO:

NATURAL DYES IN CONTEXT, PAGES 18–19
INDIGO VAT DYEING, PAGES 60–64

Navy Blue

WOOL: ALUM MORDANT

Ingredients

- *Indigo vat, see pages 60–64*
- *Wool, alum-mordanted at 8%, see page 57*
- *Neutralizing bath: ¼ tsp (1 ml) acetic acid at 20%, or a small amount of white vinegar in 2 pt (1 l) of cold water*

Method

1 Follow Step 1 of the General Method.

2 Gently immerse wet fabric for 10 minutes in the vat so as not to add any oxygen to the vat.

3 Follow Steps 3–4 of the General Method.

4 Gently remove the fabric from the vat. Oxidize in the air for 10 minutes. Make sure that the fabric remains open and flat while it is out of the vat.

5 Dip the fabric back in the vat for 10 minutes.

6 Remove from the vat and oxidize for 10 minutes.

7 Repeat Steps 5 and 6 until 10 dips and oxidizations have been completed.

8 Follow Steps 9–11 of the General Method.

VARIATION: *Try as many different fabrics in the indigo vat as you can; even man-made fabrics can sometimes produce good results.*

Sky Blue

SILK: NO MORDANT

Ingredients

- *Indigo vat, see pages 60–64*
- *Silk*
- *Neutralizing bath: ¼ tsp (1 ml) acetic acid at 20%, or a small amount of white vinegar in 2 pt (1 l) of cold water*

Method

Follow Steps 1–11 of the General Method.

VARIATION: *Dip and oxidize for differing lengths of time, varying not only the dip times but also the oxidization times. Some dyers prefer to work on short constant times, i.e., 1-minute dip and 1-minute oxidize, while others prefer to dip for 5 minutes, then oxidize for 10 minutes. It is important to record what you do, so that you can repeat if you get a really special color.*

Cyan Blue

SILK: ALUM MORDANT

Ingredients

- *Indigo vat, see pages 60–64*
- *Silk, alum-mordanted at 8%, see page 57*
- *Neutralizing bath: ¼ tsp (1 ml) acetic acid at 20%, or a small amount of white vinegar in 2 pt (1 l) of cold water*

Method

Follow Steps 1–11 of the General Method.

VARIATION: *Vary the color depth by varying the time, i.e., three 1-minute dips with three oxidizations of 1 minute.*

General Method (for Cottons)

1 Prepare the indigo vat following the instructions on pages 60–64. If there is a skin or bloom on the vat carefully remove it with a kitchen towel.

2 Gently immerse wet fabric for 1 minute in the vat so as not to add any oxygen to the vat.

3 The fabric should hang freely so all surfaces are exposed to the indigo liquid.

4 Gently move and turn the immersed fabric underneath the surface to aid even dyeing.

5 Gently remove the fabric from the vat and oxidize in the air for 1 minute. Make sure that the fabric remains open and flat while it is out of the vat.

6 Dip the fabric into the vat for another 1 minute.

7 Remove from the vat and oxidize for 1 minute.

8 Repeat Steps 6 and 7 until five dips and oxidizations have been completed.

9 Rinse well in warm water.

10 Soak in a bath of diluted acetic acid or white vinegar for 10 minutes to neutralize the caustic soda in the indigo vat.

11 Rinse well in warm water and then wash in warm water using a pH-neutral soap. Rinse well again in warm water and air-dry.

Lime Green

COTTON: AFTER-MORDANT WITH IRON

INGREDIENTS

- *Indigo vat, see pages 60–64*
- *Cotton fabric swatch, pre-dyed with weld (see page 108)*
- *After-mordant bath of iron: At 2%*
- *Neutralizing bath: ¼ tsp (1 ml) acetic acid at 20%, or a small amount of white vinegar in 2 pt (1 l) cold water*

Method

1 Follow Steps 1–8 of the General Method.

2 Immediately immerse the fabric in the after-mordant iron bath. Raise the temperature to boiling and simmer for 30 minutes.

3 Follow Steps 9–11 of the General Method.

VARIATION: *Try overdyeing a variety of different pre-dyed fabrics to see what colors can be achieved. These can be ones that you have naturally dyed yourself, or you could even experiment with store-bought natural fabrics that have patterns or stitching on them.*

SEE ALSO:

NATURAL DYES IN CONTEXT, PAGES 18–19
INDIGO VAT DYEING, PAGES 60–64

Denim Blue

COTTON: TANNIC ACID MORDANT

INGREDIENTS
- *Indigo vat*
- *Tannic acid mordant: At 8%*
- *Neutralizing bath: ¼ tsp (1 ml) acetic acid at 20%, or a small amount of white vinegar in 2 pt (1 l) cold water*

Method

1 Follow Step 1 of the General Method.
2 Gently immerse wet fabric for 5 minutes in the vat so as not to add any oxygen to the vat.
3 Follow Steps 3–4 of the General Method.
4 Gently remove the fabric from the vat and oxidize in the air for 5 minutes. Make sure that the fabric remains open and flat while it is out of the vat.
5 Dip the fabric into the vat for another 5 minutes.
6 Remove from the vat and oxidize for 5 minutes.
7 Repeat Steps 5–6 until six dips and oxidizations have been completed.
8 Follow Steps 9–11 of the General Method.

VARIATION: *You could refresh your old denim jeans in the indigo vat but do beware that the indigo can take a few washes before it is totally fixed into the jeans so could mark off when you wear them at first if you do not wash them beforehand.*

Blue-gray

COTTON: NO MORDANT

INGREDIENTS
- *Indigo vat*
- *Cotton fabric swatch, pre-dyed with madder (see page 114)*
- *Neutralizing bath: ¼ tsp (1 ml) acetic acid at 20%, or a small amount of white vinegar in 2 pt (1 l) cold water*

Method

Follow Steps 1–11 of the General Method.

VARIATION: *Try dipping and oxidizing the fabric for different periods of time to see what other color variations you can achieve.*

Pale Blue

COTTON: TANNIC ACID MORDANT

INGREDIENTS
- *Indigo vat*
- *Cotton, tannic acid-mordanted at 8%*
- *Neutralizing bath: ¼ tsp (1 ml) acetic acid at 20%, or a small amount of white vinegar in 2 pt (1 l) cold water*

Method

Follow Steps 1–11 of the General Method.

VARIATION: *Try varying the times, i.e., try a 1-minute dip and oxidize once for 1 minute to see the variation in color depth.*

Recipes

Store Cupboard Supplies

ONIONSKINS, TURMERIC, AND BLACKBERRIES ARE ALL FUGITIVE DYES, AS
THEY FADE IN LIGHT, BUT THEY ARE READILY AVAILABLE AND EASY TO USE.

General Method

Steps 1–4 vary, depending on the ingredient.
5 Stir the fabric frequently so all the surfaces pick up the dye color evenly, but make sure that the fabric remains underneath the water surface at all times.
6 During the dyeing you can check the color of the fabric by rinsing under running cold tap water and then squeezing tightly dry.

7 Place back in the dyebath if you require a stronger color.
8 When you have the color you want, rinse well in warm water and then wash in warm water using a pH-neutral soap. Rinse well again in warm water and air-dry.

Onionskins

WOOL: ALUM MORDANT

INGREDIENTS
• *Onionskins: 100–200% to dry weight of fabric*
• *Wool, alum-mordanted at 8%, see page 57*

Method

1 Place the onionskins in a saucepan. Cover with hot water and bring to the boil.
2 Simmer for 45 to 60 minutes. Cool in the saucepan.
3 Strain the onionskin water into a dyepot. Add enough warm water to allow free movement of the fabric below the water.
4 Wet the fabric and add it to the dyebath. Slowly bring to the boil over 20 to 30 minutes. Simmer for 30 to 60 minutes.
5 Follow Steps 5–8 of the General Method.

 VARIATION: *If, after 60 minutes of fully dyeing, the color is not strong enough for you, add more strained onionskin dye water to help darken the color. You can often get lots of onionskins for free by asking your local supermarket or grocery store or by picking out the skins at the bottom of the onion boxes on the shelf.*

▶ SEE ALSO:
"STORING INGREDIENTS," PAGE 136

Blackberries

WOOL: ALUM MORDANT

INGREDIENTS
- *Blackberries: 100% to dry weight of fabric*
- *Wool, alum-mordanted at 8%, see page 57*

Method
1 Place the blackberries in a saucepan. Cover with hot water and bring to the boil.
2 Simmer until soft and then strain through the mesh of some old panty hose so that no seeds remain in the strained liquid.
3 Add enough warm water to a dyepot to allow free movement of the fabric below the water. Add the strained blackberry liquid.
4 Wet the fabric and add it to the dyebath. Slowly bring to the boil over 20 to 30 minutes. Simmer for 30 to 60 minutes.
5 Follow Steps 5–8 of the General Method.

VARIATION: *Change the color by adding more or fewer blackberries. If you have missed the picking season, you can use frozen instead of fresh blackberries.*

Turmeric 1

WOOL: ALUM MORDANT

INGREDIENTS
- *Turmeric: 100–200% to dry weight of fabric*
- *Cotton, alum-mordanted at 8%, see page 57*

Method
1 Place the turmeric in a saucepan, add enough hot water to dissolve the powder, and bring to the boil.
2 Simmer for 45 to 60 minutes. Cool in the saucepan.
3 Strain the liquid through the mesh of some old panty hose into a dyepot. Add enough warm water to allow free movement of the fabric below the water.
4 Wet the fabric and add it to the dyepot. Slowly heat to just below boiling point over 20 to 30 minutes. Simmer for 30 to 120 minutes.
5 Follow Steps 5–8 of the General Method.

VARIATION: *Leave the dyebath overnight without any heat to increase the depth of color.*

Turmeric 2

COTTON: NO MORDANT

INGREDIENTS
- *Turmeric: 100–200% to dry weight of fabric*
- *Cotton*

Method
1 Place the turmeric in a saucepan, add enough hot water to dissolve the powder, and bring to the boil.
2 Simmer for 45 to 60 minutes. Cool in the saucepan.
3 Strain the liquid through the mesh of some old panty hose into a dyepot. Add enough warm water to allow free movement of the fabric below the water.
4 Wet the fabric and add it to the dyebath. Slowly heat to just below boiling point over 20 to 30 minutes. Simmer for 30 to 40 minutes.
5 Follow Steps 5–8 of the General Method.

VARIATION: *Use less powder to achieve a weaker color. Although turmeric is a fugitive color, it can produce very intense shades, which then fade to weaker ones.*

Motif Directory

DYE CAN BE USED TO INTRODUCE PATTERN TO FABRIC BY PREVENTING THE DYE FROM ACTING ON SELECTED AREAS. THE RESIST CAN TAKE THE FORM OF BINDINGS AND TIES PLACED AROUND PLEATS OR GATHERED FABRIC OR AROUND OBJECTS, WHICH ACT AS A FORM OF TEMPLATE.

Motifs can be reproduced on fabric by using batik (see page 84) or by painting or printing selected areas with a mordant or dye paste. The motifs over the next few pages can be transferred onto the fabric by either tracing the motif onto the right side of the fabric, using a lightbox, or by creating a stencil, which can be placed on the right side of the fabric and drawn around.

Designing with Pattern

One approach to fabric design is to choose a motif, or several motifs, and photocopy them several times in a variety of sizes. Keep one motif of each size as a guide for making a template and cut out the remaining motifs. Lay the motifs onto the fabric, trying various images, sizes, and combinations of size and image. Remember motifs can also be flipped or rotated. To create a template, copy the motifs onto a plastic sheet or acetate using a permanent marker. If the motif can be used as a stencil, cut out the unwanted areas. If the design is to be traced onto the fabric before wax or mordant paste is applied, then chalk or one of the many quilters' pens will ensure no permanent mark is left. Of course a design can also evolve—try positioning motifs randomly, with some hand-drawn shapes to fill any awkward spaces. The fabric can always be overdyed.

> ### PATTERN POINTER
> Use a digital camera to record your fabric designs as you try out various motif combinations.

Daisy

The application of this motif mirrors what can be seen in nature and as such will always look good on fabric.

> ### PATTERN POINTER
> After the initial dye bath, selected areas such as a flower head can be lightened by applying lemon juice. The fabric should be left to dry in a warm place or in the sun for best results.

Crown

Use only one outline to create a stencil. This motif is a useful general shape because it can be interpreted as leaves, a tulip, or used in a geometric pattern.

Lotus Flower

Use only one outline to create a stencil. This classic motif works well drawn freehand or with the aid of a stencil.

Paisley

This simple paisley design can be interpreted in a number of ways. For further inspiration of how this shape can be used, look at feather quilt stitch patterns as well as paisley fabrics.

Decorative Leaf

This motif demonstrates how any image can be used to create a geometric design.

Flying Bird

Use only one outline to create a stencil. Changing the positions of the wings in this motif animates the image. Freehand-drawn legs can also be added.

Zigzag

Even the simplest shapes can become exciting if they are rotated and repeated. This design can easily be drawn freehand.

Butterfly

Use only one outline to create a stencil. Adapt this motif by varying its scale and drawing the antennae, legs, and patterns freehand within the wing shapes.

Basketweave

This design can be reproduced using a template or can be drawn freehand. The two-color design uses a stencil template.

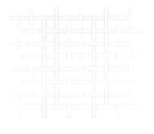
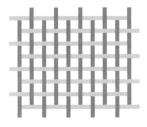

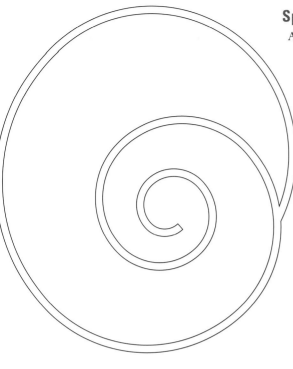

Spiral

A spiral is a very useful motif because it can be used to fill awkward spaces in most designs. Multiple spirals create an effective geometric design without sharp corners. Spirals look great drawn freehand so don't worry too much about tracing the curves accurately.

Heart

Use only one outline to create a stencil. This motif might hold another within it; why not draw a flower, leaf, or geometric pattern in the heart's center?

Leaf and Sepal

Any shape can be repeatedly outlined to create an interesting variation. The concentric lines of neighboring motifs could also be allowed to overlap.

PATTERN POINTER

If the design is to be repeated across the fabric, cut the template to the size of the repeat. Mark the position of the corners of the template onto the fabric each time the design is transferred and use these marks to reposition the template.

SEE ALSO:

INTRODUCING PATTERN, PAGE 42

Recording Data

It is absolutely essential that you keep records of all your dyeing. You may think that you will remember what dyestuff you used and with what mordant, but chances are you will forget.

	DATE	DYESTUFF USED	AMOUNT OF DYESTUFF	WEIGHT, TYPE OF FIBER	MORDANT	
5	15/03/09	Logwood	50%	1 Kilo Shetland ARAN	ALUM	
6	16/03	Cochineal	30%	1 Kilo Shetland Aran	ALUM	
7	17/03	Logwood Cochineal Exh. Bath #6	20% Logwood	1 Kilo Shetland Aran	ALUM	
8	21/03	Madder- chopped roots	100%	1 Kilo DK 20% Cashmere 40% Angora 40% Merino	ALUM	
9	23/03	Madder Exhaust Bath #8 Madder Powder Cochineal	20% Madder Powder 10% Cochineal	1 Kilo Shetland Aran	ALUM - brightened with Tin @ 3%	
10	29/03	Onion Skins- mostly yellow but some Red.	40%	1 Kilo Shetland Aran	Copper	
11	2/04	Heather collected 09/08 & dried	50%	1 Kilo DK 20% Cashmere 40% Angora 40% Merino	ALUM	
12	4/04	INDIGO		½ Kilo g # 11		
13	4/04	INDIGO		1 Kilo Merino Aran		

Keeping a Record Book

You will need a notebook and small labels for attaching to dyed fabric samples or skeins.

Any notebook will do, but the best is a looseleaf binder in which you can use heavy paper that will hold your samples. It will also enable you to add pages as you need them. You may need a punch to make proper holes to fit the paper in the binder.

Once you have your notebook, make columns for date, dyestuff used, when and where it was collected (if you collected it yourself), the amount of dyestuff used, the weight and type of fibers of fabric dyed, and what mordant (if applicable). Finally, attach a small sample of the dyed yarn, fleece, or fabric swatch. Number each entry. Then, when your yarn or fabric is dyed, washed, and dried, attach a small label that refers to the number in your record book.

Calculating Amounts

All recipes for mordanting or dyeing give percentages for the amount of mordant, additives (such as vinegar), and dyestuffs to be used. For ease of calculating:

- 2 lb, 4 oz = 1 kg
- 1 lb, 2 oz = 500 g
- 9 oz = 250 g

When calculating amounts, the base figure is the dry weight of the fiber to be dyed, which means that whatever weight of fiber is being dyed, it is called 100%. Therefore, if you are going to dye 9 oz (250 g) of fiber and the recipe calls for 50% dyestuff, you will require 4½ oz (125 g) of dyestuff.

It's much easier to work in grams than in pounds and ounces. However, if the latter is your choice, the conversion table (see right) should help you calculate amounts for both methods. If you are using pounds and ounces, when it comes to the 2% and 3% mordants (and also the 5% if doing a small amount of yarn), a good pinch or ¼ teaspoon will do since these amounts are generally only to alter the color by saddening or brightening it.

Fabric or Yarn Weight to be Dyed	Required Percentage of Dyestuff or Mordant	Required Weight of Dyestuff or Mordant
1 kg (2 lb, 4 oz)	200%	2 kg (4 lb, 8 oz)
	100%	1 kg (2 lb, 4 oz)
	50%	500 g (1 lb, 2 oz)
	30%	300 g (10½ oz)
	24%	240 g (8½ oz)
	8%	80 g (2½ oz)
	7%	70 g (2½ oz)
	5%	50 g (1½ oz)
	3%	30 g (1½ oz)
	2%	20 g (¾ oz)
500 g (1 lb, 2 oz)	200%	1 kg (2 lb, 4 oz)
	100%	500 g (1 lb, 2 oz)
	50%	250 g (9 oz)
	30%	150 g (5 oz)
	24%	120 g (4¼ oz)
	8%	40 g (1½ oz)
	7%	35 g (1¼ oz)
	5%	25 g (1 oz)
	3%	15 g (½ oz)
	2%	10 g (¼ oz)
200 g (9 oz)	200%	500 g (1 lb, 2 oz)
	100%	250 g (9 oz)
	50%	125 g (4½ oz)
	30%	75 g (2½ oz)
	24%	60 g (2 oz)
	8%	20 g (¾ oz)
	7%	17 g (½ oz)
	5%	13 g (½ oz)
	3%	7 g (¼ oz)
	2%	5 g (¼ tsp)

Safety First

NATURAL DYES ARE LESS TOXIC THAN THEIR CHEMICAL EQUIVALENTS, BUT EVEN SO, YOU STILL NEED TO BEAR SAFETY CONSIDERATIONS IN MIND. SOME DYES INVOLVE DANGEROUS SUBSTANCES, SUCH AS SODIUM HYDROXIDE, A HIGHLY CAUSTIC PRODUCT USED IN DYEING WITH NATURAL INDIGO.

The Right Clothing

At the very least, an apron, protective gloves, and goggles are advisable. A safety face mask is also a good idea. This may be either a disposable face mask or a respirator face mask, which has filters to protect you against chemicals. Refer to the safety sheets supplied with the dyes and chemicals. Remember to wear the safety clothing at all times.

Handling Dye Powders

If you are required to mix dye powder colors, always wear the correct face mask as advised in the safety sheets issued by your supplier. Mix the powders in a well-ventilated area but without a draught or breeze so that the powders do not disperse and you do not inhale them.

Handling Chemicals

Chemicals used in natural dyeing vary in the potential harm they can cause. Refer to the safety sheets issued by your supplier with the chemicals to ensure that you use these correctly and safely. Some store cupboard ingredients such as cream of tartar will not need such careful handling but it is a good idea to get into the habit of taking care at all times when handling chemicals for dyeing. If you have to handle liquid dyes or chemicals, wear safety goggles and be extra careful to ensure no splashing occurs.

Using Heat

Some recipes involve boiling the dye solutions or bringing them to temperatures as high as 160°F (70°C) or more. All the usual commonsense precautions must be observed. Think ahead and plan your work space well so that you don't have to transport hot liquids far, from the heat source to another container; don't forget to turn off irons and steamers.

Storing Ingredients

All utensils, containers, and dyeing pots should be used for dyeing only and not for cooking. It is extremely important to store all dyes and chemicals safely in airtight containers, labeled clearly with the contents and the date mixed. Keep them in a safe, dry place away from cooking areas and safely out of the reach of children, pets, and other members of the household. Check the safety sheet that is supplied as a legal requirement with all chemicals.

In Case of Accidents

Follow the guidelines on the health and safety data sheets and seek medical advice immediately.

Allergic Reactions

Some people can get an allergic reaction to some of the dyes or chemicals used in these recipes. If you think you are experiencing a reaction to any substance, consult your doctor.

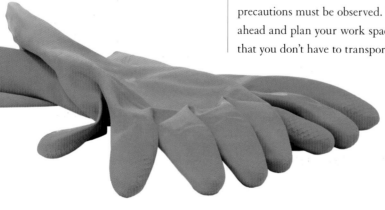

Plan Your Work Space

INVESTING A LITTLE TIME IN CHOOSING AND PLANNING
THE AREA IN WHICH YOU ARE GOING TO WORK IS WELL
WORTH THE EXTRA EFFORT. NOT ONLY WILL YOUR WORK
RUN MORE SMOOTHLY AND EFFICIENTLY, BUT YOU WILL
ALSO ENJOY IT MORE, WITH EVERYTHING TO HAND AND
ORGANIZED TO SUIT THE DEMANDS OF THE DYEING PROCESS.

Find a work space that works for you. A converted shed, barn, or studio space is ideal as it means you will not need to double up your kitchen space. Here, Eva Lambert checks on her dye vats.

Choosing Where to Work

The area you choose as your work space must be well lit and easy to clean, with your tools and materials readily to hand. Plan it in much the same way as a kitchen, so that you can dye and decorate fabrics and yarns without constantly having to move from space to space. As some of the recipes and techniques featured in this book involve leaving processes to take effect for a period of time, for example indigo dyeing, you will need a space that will allow you to leave pots, fabric, yarns, and tools out overnight, safely away from children and pets.

As your interest in dyeing grows, you may want to buy additional equipment and materials, and these will need to be stored somewhere, too. You should also ensure that you can reach all the yarns and fabrics you are dyeing and that your work surface is at a comfortable height so that you can operate without straining. Your work area will also need to be warm and well-ventilated.

Creating a Dyeing Area

If you are dyeing your fabric and yarn following most of the recipes in this book, you will need either to use your kitchen stove, or invest in a separate gas or electric heating ring to heat the dyes.

To use your kitchen stove safely, certain precautions must be followed. Do not cook or prepare food at the same time as you are working with dye; cover all food preparation areas with paper or plastic while dyeing, and never cook or prepare food using pans and other containers or utensils that have been used for dyeing.

Ideally, it is best to have a totally separate portable heating ring for fabric and yarn dyeing. This can be gas or electric, but must be big enough to comfortably hold large dye containers without any risk of them toppling over.

Creating a Work Surface

If your chosen recipe involves designing onto fabric with batik or resist methods, you will need a suitable work surface on which you can pin and tape the fabric flat. A flat work board that you can place on a table or any firm surface is ideal. The board should also be easy to clean so that it can be reused.

If you plan to do a lot of fabric designing, you can make a more durable work surface by covering a table with a plastic or PVC covering. First, cover the table with a thick blanket, pull it taut and staple it to the table. Cover this with plastic or PVC sheeting and, again, pull it taut and staple it on the underside, as shown in more detail over the page. Then cover this with a backing cloth of calico or an old clean sheet, glued in place with a thin layer of liquid gum Arabic. This backing cloth can be easily removed for washing between printing sessions. Follow the instructions over the page to make your work board.

Making a Work Board

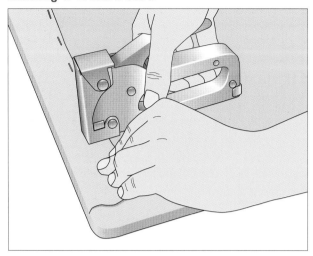

① Choose a piece of ½ in (1 cm) chipboard, blockboard, or MDF (medium density fiberboard), slightly larger than the fabric you will be printing, and cover it with a blanket. This needs to be firmly stretched over the board and secured with a staple gun (or use upholstery tacks) on the underside, leaving the work surface smooth and wrinkle-free. Stapling alternate sides of the board, work from the middle of the sides toward the corners, folding them over neatly to finish.

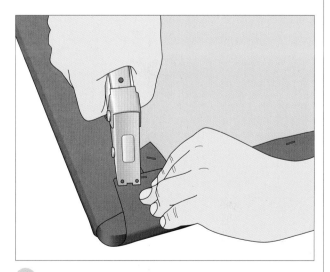

③ Work from the middle of the board outward to ensure a flat, smooth work surface.

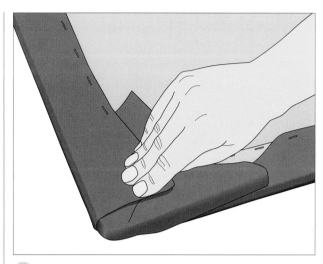

② Cover the blanket with thick plastic sheet or PVC, stretching it firmly and smoothly over the surface. Attach to the board with a staple gun or tacks.

Making a Table Cover

① Lightly gum a thick plastic or PVC sheet with a thin layer of liquid gum Arabic using a squeegee, old credit card, or spatula. Allow to dry.

② Place a sheet of calico or cheap plain white cotton as a backing cloth over the plastic or PVC and carefully steam-press onto the surface using a steam iron. Make sure there are no wrinkles because these can affect the final result of the printing.

③ Now pin your fabric to this cloth, making sure that the pins are flat against the surface but without damaging the plastic. Alternatively you can lightly iron your fabric directly onto the gum Arabic—the gum will wash off and not affect your work.

Glossary

Adjective Dyes

Dyes that require a mordant to fix the color to the fiber, yarn, or fabric.

Dyebath

The resulting liquor strained from the boiled dyestuff, or the liquor and the dyestuff in the dyepot.

Exhaust Bath

Once the initial dyeing has been completed, and your fiber, yarn, or fabric has been carefully taken out of the dyepot, the leftover liquor, which often can be used again, is called the exhaust bath.

Fast

A dye that remains on the fiber, yarn, or fabric after thorough washing and will not fade.

Fiber

Refers to the unspun fleece from sheep, goats, alpaca, etc.

Fugitive

A dye that will fade with subsequent washings or if exposed to sunlight.

Mordant

A substance, generally a metal salt, that fixes the dye to your fiber, yarn, or fabric.

Scour

To wash your fiber, generally fleece, to remove dirt and grease.

Substantive

Dyes that do not require a mordant to fix the color.

Top Dyeing

To dye one color after—or on top of—another color to produce a third color.

Wetting Out

To carefully soak your fiber, yarn, or material in warm water, preferably with a small amount of detergent, before the dyeing process is begun.

Yarn

Refers to spun yarn, either commercially or handspun.

Resources

ORDER/STORE-BOUGHT DYESTUFFS AND FIBERS

Aurora Silk
434 NE Buffalo St.
Portland, OR 97211
www.aurorasilk.com
(503) 286-4149

Creative Illuminations
AKA Gelluminations Inc.
11959 240th Ave.
Spirit Lake, IA 51360
www.creativeilluminations.com
(712) 336-4526

Dharma Trading
PO Box 150916
San Rafael, CA 94915
www.dharmatrading.com
(800) 542-5227

Earth Guild
33 Haywood St.
Asheville, NC 28801
www.earthguild.com
(800) 327-8448
Fax: (828) 255-8593

Joy of Handspinning
1925 Billings Ave.
Helena, MT 59601
(406) 431-1688

Thai Silks
252 State St.
Los Altos, CA 84022
www.thaisilks.com
(800) 722-7455

The Woolery
239 West Main St.
Frankfort, KY 40601
www.woolery.com
(800) 441-9665
Fax: (502) 352-9802

Treenway Silks
501 Musgrave Rd.
Salt Spring Island, BC
Canada V8K 1V5
www.treenwaysilks.com
(888) 383-7455

Zipper Stop
27 Allen St.
New York, NY 10002
www.zipperstop.com
(212) 226-3964

RECOMMENDED READS

AFRICAN ART
Frank Willet
Thames & Hudson
reprinted, 1988

AFRICAN TEXTILES & DYEING TECHNIQUES
Claire Polakoff
Routledge & Kegan Paul, 1980

BRIGHT EARTH: ART & THE INVENTION OF COLOR
Philip Ball
University of Chicago Press, 2001

COCHINEAL RED: TRAVELS THROUGH ANCIENT PERU
Hugh Thomson
Weidenfeld & Nicolson, 2006

ISLAMIC ART
David Talbot Rice
Thames & Hudson
revised edition, 1975

ISLAMIC PATTERNS: CARPETS & TEXTILES OF MOROCCO
Keith Critchlow
Textile Museum, Washington D.C., 1980

MADDER RED: A HISTORY OF LUXURY & TRADE
Robert Chenciner
Curzon Press, 2000

NAVAJO & HOPI WEAVING TECHNIQUES
Mary Pendleton
Studio Vista, 1974

PRIMITIVE ART
Franz Boas
Dover Publications, 1955

TIGER RUGS OF TIBET
edited by Mimi Lipton
Thames & Hudson, 1988

Index

A

Aborigines 14
accidents 136
adjective dyes 139
Alcea sp. (Hollyhock) 46
alkanet (*Alkanna tinctoria*)
 recipe for fabrics 120–121
 recipe for yarns 102–103
allergic reactions 136
Alnus glutinosa (Alder) 50
alpaca 24
alum (potassium aluminium
 sulphate) 14, 16, 17, 22, 65
 mordanting 56, 57
ammonia 56
Anthemis tinctoria (Yellow
 Camomile) 46
apron, plastic 23

B

Bambara people 14
barks
 collecting 50–51
 storing 51
basketweave motif 132
batik dyeing 76, 80, 84–85,
 130
berries
 collecting 53
 storing 53
Betula sp. (Birch) 50
Betula pubescens or *pendula*
 (Dawny birch or silver
 birch) 48
blackberries 128, 129
Blackface sheep 24
blankets 15
Bokolanfini 14
bottoming *see* top dyeing
buckets, plastic 23
butterfly motif 132

C

calculating amounts 135
Calluna vulgaris (Heather)
 46, 92–93, 111
Caltha palustris (Marsh
 marigold) 46
camel 24

cashmere 25, 32
caustic soda 23, 60, 62, 63, 64
Cercocarpus montanus
 (Mountain mahogany)
 48, 50
chemicals
 chemical dyeing 14, 15
 handling 136
chrome 56
clamping 76, 80, 81, 83
clothespins 80, 81
clothing 136
coats 15
cochineal (*Dactylopius
 coccus*) 14, 16, 25, 56
 expanded dyeing for yarn
 72, 73
 recipe for fabrics 118–119
 recipe for yarns 100–101
collecting your own
 dyestuffs
  barks 50–51
  berries 53
  flowers 46–47
  leaves 48–49
  roots 52
color 36–41
 color wheels 38
 complementary colors 39
 harmonious colors 39
 how colors make you feel
  36
 how we see color 37
 keeping a notebook 40–41
 primary colors 37, 38
 putting colors together
  38–39
 what is color? 36
compost 17
containers, plastic 23
copper (copper sulphate):
 mordanting 56, 58
Cotswold sheep 24
cotton 14, 17, 18, 31
 plain medium-weight 31
 properties 33
 scouring 35
 textured basket weave 31

top vintage cotton edging
 31
cotton poplin 19
cream of tartar 16, 17, 57
crêpe georgette 17
crimp 24
crown motif 131
cutch (*Acacia catechu*):
 recipe for fabrics 112–113
Cytisus scoparius (Broom)
 46

D

daisy motif 130
Daucus carota (Queen
 Anne's lace, Wild carrot)
 46–47
Day, Lucienne 42
decorative leaf motif 131
dhak 17
digital printing 17
dyebath 15, 25, 56, 139
dyeing techniques
 batik dyeing for textiles
  84–85
 dyeing fabric: an
  introduction 74–75
 expanded dyeing for yarn
  72–73
 indigo vat dyeing for yarn
  60–64
 mordanting 56–59
 multicolor dyeing for
  textiles 76–77
 random dyeing for yarn
  70–71
 resist dyeing fabrics with
  indigo 80–83
 tie-dyeing textiles 78–79
 tie-dyeing yarn 66–69
 top dyeing for yarn 65

E

elder (*Sambucus nigra* and
 canadensis) recipe for
 yarns 94–95
exhaust baths 56, 139

F

fabrics
 defined 13
 batik dyeing for textiles
  84–85
 choosing for dyeing 30–31
 control fabric 31
 dyeing fabric: an
  introduction 74–75
 fabric reactions 30–31
 measuring 34, 35
 mordanting 59
 multicolor dyeing for
  textiles 76–77
 overdyeing textiles 77
 preparing to dye fabric
  34–35
 properties 32–33
 recipes for *see under*
  recipes
 resist dyeing fabrics with
  indigo 80–83
 testing dyes and fabrics 31
 tie-dyeing textiles 78–79
 weighing 34, 35
fast 139
fiber: defined 13, 139
Filipendula ulmaria
 (Meadow-sweet, queen
 of the meadow) 47, 52
flax plant 33
fleece
 dyeing in large vessel 22
 preparing 27
 types of fiber 24–25
 washing 26, 27
flowers
 collecting 46–47
 estimating amounts 47
 storing 47
flying bird motif 132
folding 81
formic acid 56
Fraxinus excelsior (Ash) 51
fugitive 139
fungi 15
fustic (*Chlorophora tinctoria*):
 recipe for fabrics 106–107

index•credits

G

G-clamp 80, 81, 83
Galium verum, G. boreale (Lady's bedstraw, northern bedstraw) 47, 52
Genista tinctoria (Dyer's greenweed) 49
gloves, rubber 23
goldenrod (*Solidago* sp., especially *Canadensis* ssp.): recipe for yarns 90–91

H

handling dye powders and chemicals 136
Harris tweed 56
heat, using 136
heather (*Calluna vulgaris*) recipe for fabrics 111 recipe for yarns 92–93
Hedera helix (Common ivy) 49, 53
henna (*Lawsonia inermis*): recipe for fabrics 110
hydros 60–64

I

ikat 66, 68–69
indican 60
indigo 14, 17, 18, 19, 23, 25
recipe for fabrics 124–127
resist dyeing fabrics with 80–83
and safety 136
top dyeing for yarn 65
vat dyeing for yarn 60–64
Iris pseudacorus (Yellow iris) 52
iron (ferrous sulphate): mordanting 56, 59
iron rust 18

J

jar, airtight 23

K

"Karamatsu shibori" 18, 19
kemp 24

L

leaves 17, 19
collecting 48–49
storing 49
Ligustrum vulgare (Wild privet) 49
linen
laser-cut 31
properties 33
scouring 35
tablecloth 31
logwood (*Haematoxylum campechianum*)
expanded dyeing for yarn 73
recipe for fabrics 122–123
recipe for yarns 17, 25, 104–105
lotus flower motif 131

M

machine stitching 17
Maclura pomifera (Osage orange) 51
madder (*Rubia tinctorum*) 16, 57
expanded dyeing for yarn 72, 73
recipe for fabrics 114–115
recipe for yarns 98–99
"Maki-age shibori" 19
marbles 80, 81, 82
mask 23
meadowsweet 65
Merino sheep 24, 25
mohair 25
mordanting 56–59, 74, 77, 139
Morris, William 42
motif directory 130–133
murex shells 14
Myrica gale (Bog myrtle) 49

N

Native Americans 14
"Ne-maki shibori" 18, 19
Newton, Sir Isaac 38
niddy-noddy 28

O

onionskins 72, 73, 74, 128
overdyeing textiles 77

P

paisley motif 131
pattern 42–43
pegs 81
pH levels 34, 35
Picts 14
Populus tremula (Aspen) 49
Pteridium aquilinum (Bracken fern) 49
Pyrus malus (Apple) 51

Q

Querqus sp. (Oak) 51
quilters' pens 130

R

recipes
for fabrics
alkanet 120–121
cochineal 118–119
cutch 112–113
fustic 106–107
heather 111
henna 110
indigo 124–127
logwood 122–123
madder 114–115
safflower 116–117
store cupboard supplies 128–129
weld 108–109
for yarns
alkanet 102–103
cochineal 100–101
elder 94–95
goldenrod 90–91
heather 92–93
logwood 104–105
madder 98–99
sanders wood 96–97
weld 88–89
recording data 34, 134–135
calculating amounts 135
keeping a record book 135
repeat patterns 42–43

S

resources 140
rods 23
roots 52
collecting 52–53
storing 52
rovings 25, 27
running stitch 78

S

safety first 136
safflower (*Carthamus tinctorius*): recipe for fabrics 116–117
Salix sp. (Willow) 51
Sambucus nigra, S. canadensis (Elder) 49, 53, 94–95
sanders wood (*Pterocarpus santalinus*): recipe for yarns 96–97
scales 23
scarves 17
scouring 34–35, 59, 74, 77, 139
Shantung silk 32
shawls 16, 19
sheep 24–25
Shetland sheep 24, 25
shibori 18, 19, 32, 78
Shiva Paintstiks 17
sieve 23
silk 17, 25, 59
Indian 16, 19
preparing 26
properties 32
scouring 34–35
wild 32
silk habutai 31, 35
slivers 27
soda ash 19
sodium carbonate 35
sodium dithionite 19, 60
sodium hydrosulphate 60
sodium hydroxide 136
Solidago sp. (Goldenrod) 47, 90–91
storage 22, 47, 49, 51, 52, 53, 136
store cupboard supplies 128–129

substantive 139
sweaters 19

T
tailor's chalk 78, 81
Tanacetum vulagre (Tansy, bitter buttons) 47
tannic acid 106
tansy 65
Taraxacum officinale, T. erythrospermum (Dandelion) 47
templates, creating 130
textiles *see* fabrics
thermometer 23
tie-dyeing
  textiles 78–79
  yarn 66–69
tin (stannous chloride) 65
  mordanting 56, 59
tjanting tool 85
top dyeing (bottoming) 65, 139
tops 27
tubs, plastic 23
turmeric 74, 128, 129
tussah silk 32, 35

U
Ulex sp. (Gorse) 47
understanding the basics
  all about color 36–41
  choosing fabrics for dyeing 30–31
  core utensils 22–23
  fabric properties 32–33
  introducing pattern 42–43
  preparing to dye fabric 34–35
  preparing to dye fibers 26–27
  properties of protein fibers 24–25
  skeining yarn 28–29
urine, fixing colors with 56
Urtica dioica (Common nettle) 49

V
Vaccinium sp. (Blueberry, bilberry, blaeberry) 53
vegetable matter 17
vessels, large 22
vicuña 24, 25
vinegar 58, 63

W
waffle weave 15
water quality 35
wax resist 17, 84
weld (*Reseda luteola*) 65
  recipe for fabrics 108–109
  recipe for yarns 88–89
Wensleydale sheep 24, 25
wetting out 139
Whitby, Yorkshire 14
woad 14, 60
wood ash 56
wool 24
  heavy blanket 31
  properties 32
  scouring 34
  wool delaine 31
work space planning 137–138
  making a table cover 138
  making a work board 138

Y
yarn
  defined 13, 139
  commercial 24, 25, 26
  expanded dyeing 72–73
  handspun 24, 25, 27
  indigo vat-dyeing for 60–64
  preparing 26, 27
  random dyeing 70–71
  recipes for *see under* recipes
  skeining 28–29
  tie-dyeing 66–69
  top-dyeing 65

Z
zigzag motif 132

Credits

Quarto would like to thank Shutterstock for supplying images for this book.

With thanks to the following artists for kindly supplying work for inclusion:

- Kimberley Baxter—page 17
- Jane Callender—pages 18, 19
- Fiona Moir—pages 15, 19
- Linda Thompson—page 15
- Isabella Whitworth—pages 16, 17, 19

All other yarns are the work of Eva Lambert.
All other fabrics are the work of Tracy Kendall.

All images are the copyright of Quarto Publishing plc. While every effort has been made to credit contributors, Quarto would like to apologize should there have been any omissions or errors—and would be pleased to make the appropriate correction for future editions of the book.

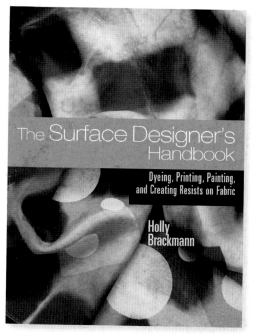

Surface Designer's Handbook
Dyeing, Printing, Painting, and Creating
Resists on Fabric

Holly Brackmann

978-1-931499-90-3

$29.95

Dyer's Garden
From Plant to Pot, Growing Dyes for
Natural Fibers

Rita Buchanan

978-1-883010-07-2

$12.95

Art Cloth
A Guide to Surface Design

Jane Dunnewold

978-1-59668-195-8

$26.95

...hand

...s the
...mmunity
...e craft.